"Masterfully weaving together psychological science and biblical wisdom, Andrea Gurney provides a practical and inspirational road map for all of us who are serious about our love story. She shows us how we can rebuild and rethink the ways we love. Don't miss out on her heartfelt message."

Drs. Les and Leslie Parrott, #1 *New York Times* best-selling authors, *Saving Your Marriage Before It Starts*

"Loving another person is beautiful but dangerous, requiring you to be both vulnerable and strong. *Reimagining Your Love Story* equips you to love others well. By combining leading research and engaging stories, neuroscience and theology, scriptural truths and practical application, Dr. Gurney helps you learn how to strengthen the relationships that matter most. I highly recommend this book!"

Peter Greer, president and CEO, HOPE International, and coauthor, *Mission Drift*

"Dr. Andrea Gurney always has a waiting list for her private practice. Once you read *Reimagining Your Love Story*, you'll understand why. In its pages, you are offered a guidebook to navigating the fairy tale while holding on to what's real, letting go of the myths without losing the wonder, and, most importantly, building upon your God-given gift of love and connection in healthy ways. I'm grateful for Dr. Gurney's work—and that readers can now access her insights without being added to a waiting list."

Laurie Polich Short, author, *When Changing Nothing Changes Everything*

"In *Reimagining Your Love Story*, Dr. Gurney effortlessly pairs foundational psychological and biblical principles in ways that are both practical and comprehensible for every audience. Whether you are single, married, dating, widowed, or divorced, this is a must-read! You will walk away with tremendous insight and tools to pursue relationships that can flourish."

Dana Allin, synod executive, ECO: A Covenant Order of Evangelical Presbyterians

"We all know that love requires work and is never as easy as the beginning of a relationship. What we often fail to address is how our perceptions and unspoken expectations create a mass of weeds that can overtake the bloom of love. Andrea Gurney brilliantly invites us to an honest, deep, and abundantly kind walk through our garden to address how sometimes even hard work is not enough. We need an honest look at what things seed division and create unfruitful conflict. This book is rich in wisdom, research, and immense humor and will restore your hope in love."

Dan B. Allender, PhD, founding president, The Seattle School of Theology and Psychology

REIMAGINING
YOUR
LOVE STORY

Biblical and Psychological
Practices for Healthy Relationships

Andrea Gurney, PhD

To Kate and Madeline,
who continually teach me
how to love well and love boldly.
To the moon and back.

Contents

The Fairy-Tale Dream

We had seventy-five minutes together. I knew the time would pass quickly, and I wanted to make sure that both Emma and Jake felt they could tell *their* version of the story.

"I'd love to hear how you two met."

They both smiled, eager to share their love story.

Emma began. "We first met when we were both in college. Jake was at Stanford and I was at Berkeley. Well, maybe you can't call it meeting," she continued with a flirtatious glance at Jake. "Jake was visiting a friend at Berkeley, and we both ended up at the same party. It was over Valentine's Day weekend, actually. Our junior year."

Jake reached over and grabbed her hand, putting it on his lap as he continued the story. "I saw her from across the way and knew I wanted to get her number before leaving that night. So I did," he said with a confident smirk.

Emma smiled. "Yes, he was successful. But—I do remember thinking, *Who is this audacious guy?* He was so . . . so sure of himself in approaching me. Little did he know, I was in a relationship already."

Jake playfully and quickly interrupted: "Come on, Em, you've got to admit. There was chemistry right away, and it was mutual."

"Oh, there's no denying that." She squeezed his hand, then looked at me. "We both immediately knew there was something there."

They were lost in the moment, remembering back to their first meeting five years ago.

"And . . . ?" I inquired.

"Oh, right," Jake continued. "Well, that was that, for the time being. I texted her occasionally, and we became Facebook friends."

"And I kept dating the other guy," Emma interjected. "But, if I'm honest with myself, Jake was often in the back of my mind. *What if he is 'the one'?* I used to wonder. I couldn't really shake it. I couldn't really shake *you*." She affectionately moved his knee back and forth as she turned toward Jake.

"Clearly I couldn't get you out of my mind all that easily either."

They enjoyed the back-and-forth, reminiscing as I listened in. He was muscular and tan—a former Stanford football player. She was taller than he was, with vibrant red hair and a smile that lit up the room. They both were articulate and talkative, yet respectful of the other person as they spoke.

"So, in short," Jake said, orienting his entire body toward me after realizing they were both facing each other on the couch, lost in the moment of their own love story, "we both ended up in San Francisco after we graduated. And as soon as we discovered we were going to be in the same city, Em broke up with that other guy, and we started dating. From the beginning—we knew we had something special."

"Yes, it really was love at first sight," Emma added. They both looked at me and grinned.

I couldn't help doing the same as I said, "It sounds like there was physical attraction from the get-go and neither of you could easily shake the image of the other."

"Exactly," Jake affirmed as Emma nodded.

"So, what brings you to my office today? Why are you two seeking couples therapy?" I inquired.

Jake sighed. "Well, we've lost some of our mojo and find ourselves struggling. Communication is hard, we fight more often, and things just don't feel right. Everything has become a bit more complicated than it used to be."

"That's often the case," I reassured them.

Messy Love

Jake was right: relationships are complicated. Fostering a healthy, intimate relationship is one of the hardest things for a human to do. And yet it is also one of the most rewarding things we can ever be a part of, integral to the way we were created. Love makes us vulnerable, but it also makes us strong. I am reminded of this every day in my work as a clinical psychologist and college professor, but also as a wife, mother, daughter, sister, and friend. As I sit with individuals, couples, and families, listening to their stories, yearnings, fears, and questions, the refrain is clear: we need one another. We are designed to be in relationships. *Imago Dei*: we are created in the image of God. And at His core, our God is relational.

But more often than not, relationships are messy. I hear it all the time:

- "I married the wrong guy. Why didn't I see it when we were dating?"
- "I'm terrified of screwing things up—my parents divorced when I was three and my mom remarried three times before she got it right."
- "I'm scared I'll never meet the right person . . . and end up all alone."
- "Things started so well between us—where did we go wrong?"
- "I look at the marriages around me and think, *No, thank you. I'll stay single!*"
- "We both share the same values. Why isn't this working?"
- "I'm worried if I keep dating him, I'm settling. But what if there is nothing better out there?"
- "How can I be sure she's the right one? I'm not even sure I'm cut out for marriage or what I should look for in a life partner."
- "I can't imagine adding kids to the picture. We've got to figure out our own stuff before we even think about starting a family."
- "I really believed that Jesus brought us together, but now I'm beginning to wonder."

If you or someone you know have faced any of these issues—welcome to this thing we call life. It's complicated, right? We are more connected than ever before in history, and yet we are lonelier. Somehow we are missing the mark on the very thing we were created for: connection and intimacy.

As we'll see over the course of this book, we are born wired as relational beings, dependent on one another for survival yet ill-equipped to establish and maintain healthy and lasting intimate relationships. Instead, we pursue "the fairy tale." We want so badly to believe there is one perfect person out there, and once we find each other, our problems will disappear, we will be "complete," and life will be easy. Or at least easier.

At the end of the day, none of us has a fairy godmother or pixie dust at our disposal. So we must do the work ourselves; we must work on understanding our own story, the cultural messages we consciously (or more often unconsciously) have believed, the places where these messages have been at variance with God's intention for our life, and the ways these things have shaped our relationships. We must work on acquiring skills to be in healthy, intimate relationships. And that is what this book is all about.

Reimagining Your Love Story is divided into three sections, each comprising four chapters. In the first section, "What's Your Once Upon a Time?" we examine both classic and emerging research and also journey through your early relationships to establish their critical role in all subsequent relationships. You'll be encouraged to reflect on how early relationships in your life have affected where you are now and what areas might need to be addressed to promote healthier relationships going forward and a stronger marriage in the future. Building on this foundation, part 2, "Deconstructing the Myths of Love," considers how some of the messages you've internalized about love, romance, and sex are straight-up fiction and an actual hindrance to developing healthy relationships. Part 2 also offers alternative ways of thinking about these topics that can lead toward fuller, more satisfying human connections. Finally, "Working Toward Happily Ever After" will equip you with skills to communicate honestly, fight fairly, make time for play, and remain curious. Although we'll be focusing on romantic relationships, the principles and practices discussed are also applicable to parent-child relationships and friendships.

Several useful sections appear at the conclusion of each chapter: "Summing Up" lists key takeaways, "So What?" offers commentary on the chapter's significance, and "Now What?" offers practical applications, questions, and exercises. Finally, if a chapter's topic resonates strongly with you, there is a "Further Reading" section at the end of the book that suggests additional resources—separated by chapter—for exploration.

To help you identify patterns and focus on opportunities for growth, I encourage you to record your thoughts, observations, and answers to specific questions and exercises as you progress through each chapter. My hope is that you will see the connections between the theoretical and practical, the day-to-day and big picture, and the seemingly mundane and necessary.

Even more, may you see that this book was born out of a desire to help you create and maintain healthy, intimate connections—kingdom relationships—that honor and glorify God. It's grounded in research and best practices of relationship science, and it includes voices of college students, young adults, mothers, fathers, sons, daughters, husbands, wives, aunts, and uncles. (All names and details of clients' stories have been changed to protect their privacy.) While many of my clients and students claim Christianity as their source of strength and hope, the relational truths explored in this book hold true for anyone seeking relational wholeness, no matter their faith. And so, my hope is that as you examine your own "once upon a time," consider the ways cultural messages have acutely influenced your perceptions, and learn simple yet profoundly transformative relational principles, you will be able to embrace your humanness and love without fear. In other words, my hope is that the pages within will help you love boldly and love well as your own story is written. This is, after all, the message we have heard from the beginning: we are to love one another (1 John 3:11).

PART ONE

What's Your Once Upon a Time?

Chapter One

Wired for Love

"I'm heartbroken and confused. I've just broken up with the man of my dreams. Or, really, he broke up with me," Samantha told me at our first meeting. "At least I think that's what just happened. I don't really even know—but it feels scary." She was twenty-six years old, smart and sophisticated, with an initial air of confidence that was admirable, especially given the circumstances.

"I don't even know who ended it—or if it's over. I just know this sucks. I'm both angry and sad. But then I have moments in which I think, 'Maybe this is for the best—maybe we should break up.' I don't know. To be honest, I'm not sure he really loves me anyway. At least not recently." She paused to catch her breath before continuing. "But when we first started dating, it was natural and easy—as if it was meant to be. Something changed a couple of months ago, though. I began to worry that Peter was interested in someone else. I don't even know what initially ignited this fear, if anything. But I became so anxious and preoccupied with the idea that Peter was going to leave me. It haunted me and, at times, kept me up at night. I'd think, *I'm not good enough for Peter*, and, *Once he really gets to know me, he's not going to love me anymore.* When I had nights like that, I couldn't help but share my thoughts with him in the morning. He'd reassure me that he loved and cared for me and wasn't interested in anyone else. And in the moment, I'd believe it. I'd believe him. But—" She stopped herself abruptly, as if she was scared to even continue her own train of thought.

"But what?" I gently probed.

"I don't know!" Samantha's tone changed from somber and pensive to annoyed and angry. She seemed fed up with her own thoughts, which she couldn't control.

We sat in silence for a moment.

"What happens in the quieter moments, Samantha? When Peter is not there to reassure you that he loves you."

"Well, that's just it. I go to a crazy place, and I don't know why. It's so incredibly infuriating. He's given me no actual reason to think he's going to leave me, yet somehow I have this horrific gut feeling that I'm going to wake up one morning and he's not going to be there. No note, no explanation, no goodbye. Just gone."

"I can see why those thoughts would both frighten and sadden you," I said with understanding. "It's as if you are worried that someone you care for very much is going to vanish, with no chance for you to even say goodbye."

Samantha's eyes filled with tears as she nodded. I breathed deeply, slightly audibly, and let the sounds of sadness fill the space.

In the Beginning

We all want to be loved. We want to have someone by our side who knows us and cares for us immensely. We want to be pursued. We want to know that someone selects us. And like Samantha, we want to rest in the security of being loved by another. This is nothing new. Since the beginning of time, humans have paired up. Adam needed Eve and Eve needed Adam—it was not good for man to be alone (Gen. 2:18). God made us to need one another. Natural selection favored people who needed people; those who were alone didn't fare as well. Humans are more social than other mammals and need to be good at cooperating to develop what neuroscientists call our "social brain."

Bottom line: we are created to be in relationship. And yet we are scared to be a part of the very thing we were created for. We are fearful of commitment. We are worried about being hurt. We don't want to be seen as needy or dependent. Yet we don't want to be alone either. We want to be chosen. We don't want to repeat the mistakes our parents made; we've witnessed the pain of divorce firsthand and don't want to go down that same path. We are skeptical about intimacy because it never seems to last. And conditioned by media and popular culture, we've been duped by cultural love myths.

This strong and deep God-given desire that we all have within is about connection. It's not about sex, selfishness, or fear. Cutting-edge research in relationship science reveals that the first and foremost instinct of all humans is to seek and maintain contact and to establish comforting connections.[1]

Attached at the Heart

Let me introduce you to John Bowlby, a British psychiatrist who worked with children in postwar Europe, pioneered the field of attachment theory, and paved the way for current research on love. In contrast with the dominant psychoanalytic wisdom of the time—which suggested that problems arose as a result of unconscious desires and fantasies—Bowlby asserted that problems were rooted in relationships with real people. He reasoned that all babies and young children would innately display what he termed proximity-seeking behavior (attachment). When he was then commissioned in 1949 by the World Health Organization to write a report on the emotional and mental health of homeless children in Europe, he found that when children were separated from their parents, they underwent three increasingly unfavorable stages of response to separation: protest, despair, and finally detachment.[2] His findings, then, confirmed his previous claims that *loving relationships are key to mental health and survival.* Drawing on Darwin's natural selection, Bowlby concluded that keeping loved ones close is an ingenious survival technique wired in by evolution. We need one another to survive.

Researchers since the time of Bowlby have confirmed that he was right when he talked about effective dependency from the cradle to the grave. Findings from many empirical studies today illuminate this fact. Perhaps the most striking results come from mortality studies conducted in industrialized nations; these studies consistently find that individuals who are emotionally and socially connected live longer, healthier lives.[3] Social connections reduce illness and relapse in individuals with preexisting medical and psychological conditions. Whether it's depression, schizophrenia, Alzheimer's, cardiovascular disease, obesity, diabetes, or cancer, we do better when we are in supportive relationships. And then there's married folks; people who are in a *satisfying* marriage live longer and have fewer psychiatric problems, a decreased risk of infection, quicker recovery from injury, and a lower rate of mortality following a life-threatening illness than those who are unmarried.[4]

★ ★ *Individuals who are emotionally and socially*
★   *connected live longer, healthier lives.*

Additionally, those who feel connected and supported fare better in the face of threat, danger, and terror. Captors have used social isolation as a means of torture for decades. And the unit of survival in concentration camps was a pair—in other words, interpersonal bonding, social reciprocity, and sharing with another victim were sources of strength and survival among inmates in the Nazi concentration camps.[5] Is it any wonder, then, that one of the best predictors of recovery for children who have been sexually abused is whether or not their mothers believed and supported them?[6] Similarly, the best predictor of whether or not an individual will overcome trauma is what happens afterward—namely, can they seek comfort in the arms of another? Secure attachments are a natural buffer and antidote against threat, terror, helplessness, and meaninglessness—for when we have somebody beside us, the darkness is less terrifying. In other words, a deep sense of belonging results in the taming of our fear.

Consider the promise of connection Jesus left with His disciples before He prepared to return to the Father: "I am with you always, to the very end of the age" (Matt. 28:20). In the same way, God tenderly reassures the nation of Israel in the Old Testament: "Do not fear, for I am with you; do not be dismayed, for I am your God. I will strengthen you and help you; I will uphold you with my righteous right hand" (Isa. 41:10). And God offers the same reassurance to us. He is here. Present. Always. Thousands of years later, scientific studies affirm the truth of God's promise: we are made for deep relationship.

There is a protective power of relationships. We are designed to love a few precious others who will protect us through the trials and tribulations of life. As researcher and psychologist Sue Johnson writes, "Sex may impel us to mate, but it is love that assures our existence."[7]

Think about it. Think about your own life. From the moment you entered this world, you were in a relationship. You interacted with those around you. As a newborn, you imitated the faces of your caregivers; you learned to open your mouth and make your eyes big and raise both your eyebrows, imitating the look of excitement and delight that you saw reflected in your caregiver's face. We learned as infants that a smile brought positive attention, so we smiled more. We quickly found out that when we cried, someone responded. And when our parents made a funny face or cooed, we waved our arms, kicked our legs, and babbled back at them. And round and round it went, in a two-way feedback loop.

✦ We were created in the image of a triune God, whose very nature is relational.

I don't expect you to remember your earliest days. But if you are among the 65 percent fortunate enough to have a secure attachment with your primary caregivers, then that's what your feedback loop looked like. I like to think of it as a dance—two people holding each other close and seamlessly engaging with one another, mutually taking turns, gently leading and following, respectful of each other's space but also not afraid to become one. It's an automatic and innate call-and-response system that is wired into our brains and nerves to keep us emotionally attached to each other. It's an emotional dialogue that is absorbed in the beginning days of our lives—before we can even hold our head up on our own, let alone speak words. It's our first instinct—to make contact and to connect. And considering that we were created in the image of a triune God, whose very nature is relational (in fact, C. S. Lewis described the relationship between the three persons of the Trinity as "a kind of dance"[8]), this makes complete sense.

Whom Do You Run To?

Picture this. You are at a family reunion. And let's pretend—if this isn't your reality—that your extended family is bursting at the seams with kids ages five and under. There's a big game of hide-and-seek going on, with running, chasing, and happy squeals filling the air. Until *boom*, *crash*, and *ouch*: two kids collide head-on and bounce off each other, falling to the ground with a thump and simultaneous tears. What happens next? That's right—they scan the crowd to find their person. And although family surrounds them—aunts, uncles, grandmothers, and grandfathers—they won't suffice. They are looking for that *one specific person*. And as soon as they find Mama or Daddy, they run toward them.

No matter what our age, most of us have a certain person we run to. Whether we've just found out about a grad school acceptance, a work promotion, devastating news of our mom's cancer, or that our fiancé wants out, there are a select few that we turn to and confide in. They are the ones we seek comfort from. God has given us one another to be a shelter from the storm.

For some of us, however, we hesitate. We're not so sure anyone can be trusted. We've been hurt too badly in the past, and it seems too risky to depend on others. Or we've learned to rely on ourselves because—at the end of the day—that's all we've really got.

Undoubtedly, life experiences and the collateral damage of humanity's brokenness have taught us different things, and attachment looks different for some of us. Perhaps you didn't have a reliable, stable caregiver that consistently met all your needs. Maybe your mother experienced postpartum depression. Or your father turned to alcohol as a way to cope when children came along. Perhaps you were in foster care for the first couple years of your life. Maybe genuine love and care was expressed but because of personality differences or temperament, the message was lost in translation. Or maybe both of your parents were too busy working to really pay attention to you. The question then becomes, Did you still form healthy attachments?

Mary Ainsworth was a psychologist who asked that question in the late 1960s. She was a student of Bowlby's and was interested in individual differences in children's attachment. Do all of us attach in the same way? And is attachment always positive? Remember, according to Bowlby, we all form attachments; it's nature's plan for the survival of the species after all. Ainsworth, however, built on Bowlby's work and found that not all of us form *healthy* attachments.

Ainsworth's classic experiment is known as the Strange Situation, a series of eight episodes in which she covertly observed mothers interacting with their twelve- to eighteen-month-olds.[9] But to add a different variable, she'd throw a random stranger into the mix and then ask the mother to leave the baby alone with the stranger for three-minute episodes. Ainsworth was interested in what occurred when the mother departed and when she returned (the "reunion"). Did the baby notice when the mom left the room? Was the little one distressed, or did she readily separate and explore the toys in the room? Did he engage with the stranger, or was he cautious? And when the mom returned, did the baby go to the mother for comfort? If so, did the baby *actually receive* comfort? Based on her results, Ainsworth described three attachment styles: *secure, insecure-ambivalent, insecure-avoidant*. One of Ainsworth's colleagues later added a fourth style, insecure-disorganized/disoriented.

- *Secure attachment*: These were the babies who were content in the presence of their mom, distressed when she left, and comforted and calmed by her return.
- *Insecure-ambivalent*: The most significant observation for these babies occurred during the reunion episode: the baby went to the mother for comfort, just like the securely attached baby did, but then pushed their mother away. Even if genuine comfort was offered in the moment, the child couldn't trust it and communicated, "I need you—I need help from you—but I can't trust you to give it."
- *Insecure-avoidant*: These babies were okay with the stranger, and they showed no signs of distress when the mother left the room (as if they didn't even notice) and little interest when the mom returned. These babies had learned—at an early age—to fend for themselves.
- *Insecure-disorganized/disoriented*: These babies had contradictory responses and appeared to be emotionally unstable. Some approached the mom but then froze or overtly displayed fear. At times they had tense, jerking movements and appeared to dissociate.

All Grown Up

You might be asking, "And so? What does my early relationship with my mother or father have to do with the way I engage in intimate relationships now? Does it really make a difference?" These are all fair questions! And here's the thing: we all developed mental models based off of our early relationships that are embedded into the very architecture of our brains. In other words, in our earliest days we internalized an image of what relationships look like and how they work. And we learned, dependent on the response and availability of our parents, whether or not we were valuable and worthy of care. If our cries and needs were consistently met with a comforting response, we internalized a sense of worthiness and competence. But if no one came when we cried and reached out—or if they were inconsistent in coming to our side—we learned to be skeptical of relationships and, moreover, people; they can't always be trusted.

In our earliest days we internalized an image of what relationships look like and how they work.

We call this our internal working model. It's a representational image of our own value based off the way we were treated when we were young. The internal working model is a set of expectations, inscribed in our brain outside of our conscious awareness in that first year, and lays the foundation for the way in which we relate to the world.

Here are some questions for you to think about from your own history.[10] I'd encourage you to write down answers to these, either now or once you finish this chapter. In answering these questions, you can start to form an awareness of how you might have internalized ideas about attachment at a young age, and how that might continue to affect the way you approach relationships today.

1. Describe your relationship with your parents as a young child, starting from as far back as you can remember.
2. To which parent did you feel the closest and why? Why doesn't this feeling exist with the other parent?

3. When was the first time you remember being separated from your parents?
   a. How did you respond? Do you remember how your parents responded?
   b. Are there any other separations that stand out in your mind?
4. In general, how do you think your overall experiences with your parents have affected your adult personality? Are there any other aspects of your early experience that you consider a setback to your development?
5. What is your relationship with your parents like currently?

⁎⁎⁎ *There is a family legacy of sorts regarding attachment styles.*

The research behind these questions indicates that attachment styles remain consistent over the years. So if a child had an ambivalent attachment style in childhood, that same style is evident in their adult relationships. Furthermore, if there was attachment rejection or trauma in the mother's childhood, her relationship with her child is characterized by similar attachment issues. In other words, there is a family legacy of sorts regarding attachment styles.

★ ★ ★

My work with Samantha continued. We picked up where we'd left off—with the unrelenting fear and worry that her person, Peter, was going to leave her unexpectedly.

"Samantha, can I change course a bit and ask you to tell me briefly about your family of origin?" I inquired of her.

"Sure. I'm happy to talk about something different." What she saw as a change of subject I saw as an integral piece to the puzzle. And integral it was indeed. I learned that Samantha's mom died after battling cancer when Samantha was four years old. Samantha and her older brother were raised primarily by their father, who purposely chose—despite opportunities to the contrary—not to get remarried until Samantha was in high school.

"In some ways, I don't know any different since I was so young when my mom died. Most of my memories are of my dad, my brother, and me. And my dad . . . he's a rock star." Her face lightened, perhaps for the first time that hour, as she recalled times with her dad. She spoke of camping trips, wrestling, surfing, and biking with her dad.

"Sounds like your dad loved doing things with you and Jeremy and did his best to move on, if you will, as a family of three."

"Yes, I don't think he wanted to dwell on the loss of my mom. Or if he did, he certainly didn't share it with us too much."

"So, what do you remember about saying goodbye to your mom? Or even processing her death?" I asked.

"What do you mean?"

"How did you say goodbye?" I thought I'd start with the concrete—the content—and then move to the process.

"I didn't."

I looked at her with curiosity; she continued.

"One night mom got really sick, unexpectedly. It was the middle of the night so my dad called my grandma, and she came over to be with Jeremy and me while he took mom to the ER. She died that night." Samantha remained stoic as she shared.

"And so you woke up in the morning and . . . ?"

"We were told that mom was at a doctor's appointment and would be back soon. So off to preschool I went. I remember getting home from school and running into the house, down the hallway right to my mom's bed. And I distinctly remember feeling panicked and confused when the bed was not only empty but the sheets and covers were gone. It was just a bare mattress." Samantha's demeanor changed; she was no longer telling the story—she was there, as an almost-five-year-old, standing frozen at her mother's empty bedside. Her eyes became big and wide as they filled with moisture. She sat motionless on the couch. It was as if she was in a trance, reexperiencing the trauma and loss that occurred twenty-two years prior.

You could hear a pin drop.

Then her head fell into her arms, her feet drew up onto the couch with her knees touching her forearms—in a fetal position—and she began to sob. "I never got to say goodbye . . . I never got to say goodbye. I never got to say goodbye to my mom."

Adult Attachment Styles

Samantha experienced a tragic loss during her childhood. At a young age, she lost her "person"—her emotional bedrock. And although she was close with her dad, her primary caregiver literally disappeared from her life suddenly and unexpectedly. As I learned during our work together, she never processed the death of her mother; they just "moved on with life," almost as if it never happened. One day her mother was there; the next she was not. Talk about unpredictable. She had a caregiver who was attuned and responsive to her needs—and then unavailable. Is it any wonder she was now preoccupied with the fear that one day she was going to wake up and Peter would be gone?

Our childhood attachment styles impact our adult relationships and, without awareness and intervention, insecurities from our early years can remain with us as adults. Children with an insecure-ambivalent attachment style, for example, often grow up to have preoccupied attachment patterns. As adults, they seek reassurance from others, yet self-doubt continues to persist. They are worried, like Samantha was, that their partner is going to stop loving them, reject them, or perhaps simply disappear from their life. And so, in an attempt to feel safe, they become clingy and dependent on their partner; this overly clingy behavior that results from their neediness and insecurity tends to push their partner away. Because they grew up distrustful of their inconsistent caregivers, they almost anticipate abandonment and look for signs that their partner is losing interest. In a way, they end up seeking a sense of security at the expense of emotional intimacy.

✦✦✦ When secure adults are in a romantic relationship, they can experience both togetherness and solitude.

Secure adults, on the other hand, do not doubt that their partner is a safe haven. Just like children when their parents served as a secure base from which they ventured out and explored the world—knowing there was a safe haven to return to—the same security carries over. As adults, they feel confident and connected and are more satisfied in their relationships. When secure adults are in a romantic relationship, they can experience both togetherness and solitude; there is freedom within a safe connection. Additionally, secure adults are able to offer support when their partner feels distressed. They also go to their partner for comfort when they themselves feel worried or hurt. Their relationship tends to be honest, open, and equal, with both people feeling independent yet loving toward each other. Their working model consists of the view that "others are helpful" and "I am worthy of respect."

And then there is the adult version of Ainsworth's insecure-avoidant attachment style; this is known as "dismissive." These are the adults who tend to be distant and independent, pretending as if they don't have any needs to be met. It's easier and more familiar for them to deny the importance of love and connection and detach from loved ones. This pseudo independence is both an illusion and defense mechanism. (Remember, as children they had to detach and fend for themselves in order to survive, so what was once a healthy coping skill becomes an unhealthy defense mechanism.) Often as adults they are psychologically defensive and can shut down emotionally. Even in heated or emotional situations, they are able to turn off their feelings and not react. For example, if their partner is distressed and threatens to leave them, they might respond by saying, "I don't care." Additionally, adults with a dismissive attachment style tend to take on the role of caring for themselves and consequently are overly focused on their own needs and comforts. At the end of the day, though, their internal working model consists of the beliefs that "I am unworthy," "I am unacceptable," and "I am unlovable."

Lastly, there is the fearful attachment style in adults whose childhood was defined by frightening and unpredictable behavior displayed by their primary caregiver. This corresponds to the fourth childhood attachment category: insecure-disorganized/disoriented.[11] These are adults who have incredibly tumultuous and often dramatic relationships, characterized by their own unpredictable moods and fears. They are both afraid to get close and worried about being distant. This tension between their fears of intimacy and abandonment leads them to cling to their partner when they feel rejected, and feel trapped by their partner when they are close. And so they are overcome by intense feelings and emotional anxiety, feeling as if there is no escape. They often feel overwhelmed by emotional storms that are unpredictable, even to themselves. The working model from which they view relationships may sound something like this: "I need to go toward this person to get my needs met, but if I go too close, they will hurt me." The person they want to run to for safety is the same person they are terrified of. This working model provides them with no organized strategy to get their needs met.

As you can see, our internal working model embodies either a secure, confident attachment (based on the dependability and proximity of our caregiver) or an insecure, anxious stance (resulting from an unavailable, inconsistent caregiver). It depends on the history of our actions and interactions with our primary caregiver. And in turn, attachment style helps ground our sense of self; a secure attachment leads to a sense of competence, mastery, and a healthy self-image in adulthood, whereas an insecure attachment causes us to question our self-worth and value. The underlying assumption, then, in applying attachment theory to later relationships is the notion that the attachment bond continues throughout life based on these internal working models developed in our early years.

★ ★ Curative, reparative relationships not only heal us but also grow and change us.

Although we cannot erase our childhood experiences and subsequent attachment style, we can take steps toward change. Awareness is the first step. Acknowledging your attachment style means recognizing not only your role in a relationship but also how your insecurities are impacting it. By identifying the emotions that arise when you feel insecure, you can learn ways to regulate them through prayer, mindfulness (discussed in chapter 12), and cognitive behavioral practices (see the "Now What?" section at the end of this chapter). Taking time to study past relationships means you can break old emotional patterns and behaviors, setting a new course for current and future relationship dances. And it is precisely within this new dance that your attachment style can be reshaped—curative, reparative relationships not only heal us but also grow and change us.

★ ★ ★

Samantha and I sat in the sorrow that filled the room. She never had a chance to say goodbye to her mother. There she was, an almost-five-year-old girl, coming home from preschool excited to snuggle and share her new song with her mom, and she was met with a bare mattress, soon to be followed by rooms full of people, some familiar, some strange. But none were her mother.

And here she was, a twenty-six-year-old woman, who had been in a loving relationship with a man but living in the worry that one unforeseen day that person too would disappear from her life.

Indeed, our early relational experiences are embedded in the architecture of our brain and lay the foundation for the way we experience the world. And from cradle to grave, when we reach out our arms for help, we want to rest in the assurance that someone is going to pick us up. We are, after all, wired to love.

Summing Up
- Universally, humans have an innate need to establish connection with one another; this is a lifelong survival technique hardwired by God into each of us!
- Early relationships are incredibly important as we form attachments— innate emotional bonds. Our attachment to primary caregivers has a lasting impact on child development and future relationships as we develop mental models that guide the way we relate to others.
- Attachment styles include:
  » Secure
  » Insecure-ambivalent
  » Insecure-avoidant
  » Insecure-disorganized/disoriented
- When we feel secure and confident in relationships—in other words, when we know someone has our back—we are more likely to explore the world around us.

So What?
Understanding our innate wiring and attachment style offers insights into adult relationships.

By examining the importance of early relational experiences, we understand how foundational they are for later intimate relationships. Our brief review of both classic and cutting-edge research in the field of attachment and child development illustrates how deeply love is embedded in relationships and how it is necessary for survival.

With this understanding, we can review our own early relationships and consider the patterns, pitfalls, and strengths within our adult relationships. Considering our own attachment style equips us to critically examine our posture—reactions, insecurities, fears, and responses to conflict—all with the goal of developing healthy relationships.

Now What? Practical Applications

- If someone disappoints you or betrays your trust today, how do you respond? If you pull away, go silent, or retaliate in some way, what might you be able to do differently?
- How were you comforted as a child? What did this teach you about emotional interactions? About love? Think through how you give and receive comfort.
- If you are in a relationship currently, discuss your answers to the five questions in the "All Grown Up" section with your significant other. Then have him or her also answer the questions. Can you see connections or patterns related to your current relationship functioning?
- Are there any childhood hurts or wounds that may underlay current behaviors and beliefs that are keeping you stuck or fueling problems in your intimate relationships?
- What is your image of God? Does God resemble either one of your parents? If so, how? Think about ways your views of God may limit your understanding of who He really is.
- Be aware of your insecurities in your relationships. What are you afraid of? What do you worry about? Be mindful of the ways they preoccupy your thoughts at times (even subconsciously). Awareness is often the first step to change.
- When your insecurities come to the forefront of your mind, replace them with "I'm okay, it's okay" and then "I am worthwhile" as you

take three deep breaths. You can also use statements such as "God loves me, God knows me, and God cherishes me."

- Practice self-care as a way to remind yourself that you are worthy and valuable! And remember: God loves you; He chose you (John 15:16). God knows you; He calls you by name (Isa. 43:1). God is with you; you are safe in Christ (Josh. 1:9).

CHAPTER TWO

Monkey See, Monkey Do

"He worked hard and provided for us; that was his role. And my mom—she was the one who took care of our needs." Michael was matter-of-fact as he spoke about his family. "We were a close family and I always felt supported, especially by my mom. My dad wasn't around as much. But when he was, I remember wanting to impress him. I wanted him to approve of everything I was doing."

I smiled and nodded. "Sounds like you really looked up to your dad."

"Yeah. And I still do," he was quick to reply.

"Yes, I had that sense." It was only our second session together, and I still had a lot to learn about the twenty-one-year-old who sat nervously on the edge of the couch in front of me.

"Can you tell me what you appreciate about your dad?"

"Oh man—he's a hard worker. And it's paid off. He's incredibly success-ful and respected in his field. He's definitely made a name for himself. He's done well financially . . . always provided for us, took us on great vacations."

"And what about emotionally? What is your relationship with your dad like?" I asked.

"He just wants me to be happy. My mom has told him that I'm having a hard time, putting a lot of pressure on myself academically and with relationships. He just wants what's best for me. But neither of them know how bad it really is—my anxiety, that is. And all of the partying and drinking and stuff . . ." Michael's voice trailed off. Shame and disappoint-ment, along with tears, filled his eyes.

Michael was the oldest of four and the only son. His dad was a very successful vascular surgeon and, from the impression I got, a pragmatic yet larger-than-life man of few words. His mom had been a stay-at-home mom and was just returning to graduate school to pursue a writing career. Michael spoke of them both fondly, although it was clear he had more of an emotional connection with his mother.

"I imagine both of your parents want what's best for you, Michael, and it hurts them to see you hurting. It seems you are carrying quite a heavy load on your shoulders, and that one way you escape is by partying."

He nodded and muttered, "Definitely."

Michael was attractive, athletic, smart, and kind. From the looks of it, everything was going his way. I barely had to scratch the surface, though, to see that Michael struggled with anxiety and depression.

He spoke of being plagued by his own thoughts, as if he could never stop the tape from running in his head. He worried what others thought of him, was fearful that he wasn't going to "make it" in his job, and was waiting for his girlfriend to break up with him. He was ashamed of his lifestyle and spoke about the mask he hid behind.

"All my friends think I've got it together, but really—I'm a disaster. I can't make it through the weekend without getting hammered, and I've cheated on my girlfriend twice already. It's bad. And I can't sleep at night unless I take a pill."

In our sessions together, Michael was honest and open. But outside of these walls, he had an image to keep up. And I was worried he was going to spontaneously combust in the process. He was putting an exorbitant amount of pressure on himself as he faced graduation and life beyond college, and he was becoming increasingly anxious and self-deprecating. What used to be a source of support and strength—his faith in God—had become yet another area of his life that he had "screwed up," another way that he had disappointed himself and his parents.

"When I lie awake at night, I try praying. But that's a joke. I know I'm going to keep going down this path, so why am I even asking God for help? It's all a facade. It's bad."

"It sounds hard. And frightening." There was a long pause. "It sounds as if you're even feeling estranged from God?"

Michael nodded as he held back tears. And then his tone shifted. "Really, it's such a joke. Why can't I just get my act together? I know I've got a lot going for me. I live in a beautiful place; I have a loving family; I've got a job lined up after graduation. I've got a girlfriend that most guys would love to have. What's wrong with me? I *should* be able to pull myself up by my own bootstraps."

"Whose voice is that in your head?" I asked.

"Oh—that's what my dad would say," Michael quickly responded. "I can hear his voice now: 'Just work harder, son.' 'Come on, now.' Or 'Get over it.' 'Figure it out.' Those were his rules to live by. And this—all of this stuff I have going on—I *should* just get over it."

As I listened to Michael, I developed a deeper understanding of why he felt trapped and tormented by his own thoughts. The person he had looked up to—literally and figuratively—for the past twenty-one years wouldn't tolerate anxiety, let alone depression. Michael was battling both, and pulling himself up by his own bootstraps wasn't working. In many areas of his life including his love life, his fear of failure, coupled with the internalized belief that stoicism is a sign of strength, prevented him from being vulnerable and honest. He was unnecessarily going it alone.

Bandura and Bobo

Albert Bandura is one of the world's most influential psychologists; some believe he's the greatest living psychologist today. Bandura wanted to know how much of what we do and feel is learned from other people. To explore this question, he designed what would become a classic experiment. Imagine this: a clown-like, inflatable, five-foot-tall plastic toy named Bobo that, when hit, falls down but immediately bounces back to an upright position. In this study, children watched an adult beat up the Bobo doll—pummeling it, kicking it across the room, hitting it on the head with a mallet, and bombarding it with balls—and then the children were left on their own to play with whatever toys they wanted.[1] (It's important to note the room was full of many enticing toys.)

What did the children do? Nearly every one mimicked the violent and aggressive behavior of the adult they had seen. The closest imitations occurred when the child observed an adult of their same sex. Even more remarkable was that *eight* months later, 40 percent of the same children reproduced the violent behavior they had seen months earlier when they were brought back into the playroom with the Bobo doll.

Bandura's Bobo doll experiment led to the development of *social learning theory*, which states that learning takes place in a social context and can occur solely through observation. In other words, we don't necessarily need reinforcements, verbal instruction, or practice to learn something. We can simply observe someone else's behavior and, as a result, reproduce similar behavior. I think of it as "monkey see, monkey do." Not surprisingly, we are more likely to imitate someone if we perceive them to be competent or attractive. (Clearly Hollywood is aware of these research findings.)

> *We can simply observe someone else's behavior and, as a result, reproduce similar behavior.*

Countless studies have been done since Bandura's 1961 experiment and, almost sixty years later, his theory not only holds true but also applies to modeling viewed on a screen.[2] In other words, watching violence in a movie, video game, or on a television show impacts us just as powerfully as witnessing it live. Social learning theory has also been applied to relational aggression and dating violence; researchers have found that when aggression has been modeled in our family of origin, we are more likely to be victims and perpetrators of aggression in dating relationships.[3]

This has powerful implications for all of us and is certainly relevant for our romantic relationships. So much of what we internalize in childhood—whether it's implied, hidden, or overt messages, behaviors, beliefs, or values—reveals why we exhibit certain behaviors in our adult relationships and how, in turn, these behaviors affect the ways we interact and engage with our partners. Additionally, social learning theory suggests that in all areas of our lives, what goes in comes out. Who we spend time with is who we will become more like. Talk about needing to choose our partners wisely! Bandura's research gives insight into why

Scripture admonishes us to be intentional about who we imitate—we are to be imitators of God, walking in the way of love, modeling and focusing on Christ's sacrificial love as we love one another (Eph. 5:1–2). We are to center our minds and hearts on what is true, noble, right, pure, lovely, admirable, and praiseworthy (Phil. 4:8).

✱✱ *Who we spend time with is who we will become more like.*

Social learning theory is especially poignant for children, as they do not have the same capacity to reflect or self-modulate. Children not only imitate but they also begin to *identify* with modeled behaviors. Often without knowing it, or even wanting to, they have assumed a similar way of thinking, acting, or even feeling. Yes, feeling. Research indicates that by watching adults handle their own feelings, children pick up strategies for how to regulate their own emotions. When a parent is warm, patient, talks through and processes emotions, a child learns to do the same, and their capacity to handle stress is strengthened.[4] On the other hand, when parents have difficulty controlling their own emotions, children develop problems in managing emotions, which leads to psychological maladjustment.[5]

And such was the case with Michael. He was now identifying with the behaviors, values, beliefs, and attitudes he observed in his dad. These messages—work hard and succeed, no matter what; be strong, always; overcome any obstacle in your way; financial provision trumps emotional connection—had now become his own subconscious, internal messages. The pressure to succeed and overcome—and appear competent and assured in the process—was not only leading to stress and anxiety but was also hindering his ability to be real and therefore intimate with his girlfriend.

★ ★ ★

"So it's your dad's voice in your head, then, urging you to get over it?" I gently asked.

Michael nodded.

"Anyone else?"

"What do you mean?" There was a confusion and sincerity in Michael's eyes.

"Oh—I'm just wondering if it's solely your dad's voice."

"I think so," Michael responded. And then there was a long pause.

"Do you believe it?"

Michael slowly began to nod. "I think so . . ."

I, too, nodded as our eyes met in contemplation and sorrow.

"Perhaps it's more of my own voice. I've become my dad in that way," Michael added. "I'm my own worst critic."

I used Michael's line as I quietly responded, "I think so."

Rewind and Rewrite

Whether we'd like to admit it or not, we all have a voice in our head. At times, it might be loud and clear, and we can laugh and identify with it: "I sound just like my mom!" At other times, it might be a quiet, maybe even painful, whisper that we barely realize is there. The truth is that over a lifetime, we've had less-than-perfect role models and absorbed thousands of both positive and negative messages from our caregivers, communities, and culture. We've seen and heard hard things, and we've taken them to heart.

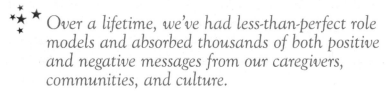 *Over a lifetime, we've had less-than-perfect role models and absorbed thousands of both positive and negative messages from our caregivers, communities, and culture.*

What do we do with these scripts seemingly embedded in our minds? How do we filter and rerecord the harmful messages we've received? The first step is to realize that these messages exist. We need to be cognizant of our all-too-familiar, often subconscious, underlying assumptions and beliefs. Research indicates that our minds are powerfully working even when we don't realize it. The more we are exposed to a message, the more likely we are to believe it as true; this occurs automatically (which is frightening if you stop and think about it!).

Once we've identified our internalized messages and recognized our underlying beliefs, we need to pay careful attention to the ways in which they impact us. In other words, we need to engage in what psychologists call self-monitoring. We need to ask, *How do these beliefs color my view of myself, others, and relationships? How do they impact my behaviors?* Lastly, after bringing these internalized beliefs and subsequent behaviors to light, we need to critically challenge them, weighing them against what we know to be true—God's Word. We need to consciously choose whether to embrace the old but familiar messages or to replace them with healthier alternatives.

★★★ *Your internalized messages are as unique as your childhood and could impact your relationships in any number of ways.*

In Michael's case, he needed to recognize the ways he hid his insecurities from his girlfriend for fear of being seen as weak or, worse yet, dependent. Self-monitoring meant actively choosing vulnerability and intimacy over a stoic facade. Michael's mantras became "I am doing my best" and "Vulnerability is strength."

Your internalized messages are as unique as your childhood and could impact your relationships in any number of ways. If upon self-assessment, you realize these messages are holding you back from healthy relationships, it's time to hit reset and work with a friend, mentor, or therapist on a plan to implement new, healthy patterns.

★ ★ ★

Michael was tenacious and stubborn. He held firmly to the belief that he should be able to pull himself up by his bootstraps and "get over it." Work hard and move on. Failure wasn't an option; it certainly wasn't something he had seen modeled in his family. Talking about his weaknesses, especially with someone like his girlfriend, was a huge faux pas. These thoughts motivated and paralyzed him. Over many weeks and months, he came to see how prevalent—albeit subconscious—and detrimental they were. They led to sleepless nights and anxiety, unattainable relation-ship expectations, and plummeting self-esteem.

Eventually Michael went from merely recognizing that something had to give to knowing, believing, and acting on it. He began to consciously choose to reclaim the words he knew as truth: "But [Jesus] said to me, '*My grace is sufficient for you, for my power is made perfect in weakness*'" (2 Cor. 12:9, emphasis added).

Summing Up

- Social learning theory states that people can learn new things by observation. Bandura's theory still carries weight today as countless recent research studies suggest that we learn by observing.
- Heard and implied messages, coupled with behaviors, impact us. This not only includes live modeling but also messages in movies, books, television, music, the internet, and video games. We imitate all these messages.
- Bandura's study supports the Bible's admonition to meditate on what is good, noble, and right and to turn away from evil, that we may become imitators of Christ (Phil. 4:8; Ps. 37:27; Eph. 5:1–2).
- Children are especially impacted by what they see and hear. Not only do they imitate behaviors but they also identify with the messages they observe. In other words, children assume a similar way of think-ing, acting, and feeling—they internalize the messages as their own.

So What?

Examining the behaviors—both nonverbal and verbal—modeled by our primary caregivers in our early years lends insight into our current ways of thinking and acting.

As children, we look to those around us to learn about the world—about love, work, family, friendships, and values. We imitate what we see and begin to make it our own; this process occurs automatically, even without our awareness. As adults, we are more equipped to cognitively sort through messages and behaviors, incorporating some and rejecting others.

Whatever our age, we are influenced by our surroundings—what we see, hear, read, and watch. Given the reality of social learning theory, we need to be intentional and aware of the messages we take in all the time, all around us. We can then weigh the messages against what we know to be true—God's Word—and the goals that we have for ourselves in relationships, and consciously choose whether to embrace these messages or to replace them with healthier alternatives.

Now What? Practical Applications
- Make a list of the behaviors you observed in your family of origin, especially from your same-sex parent, during your childhood. Are these behaviors you want to emulate?
- What messages did you internalize as a result of these observed behaviors? Write the messages down. Do you believe these messages today? How might they be limiting you?
- Think through who your role models have been—both as a young child and currently. What do they have in common? What's different? What are the traits of your role models you'd like to emulate in your life today?
- Consider Jesus as your role model. As He was arguably the world's most effective teacher, what can you learn about relationships from His example? (If you're unsure where to start, see Matthew 5:1–12.)
- Think through the messages—both verbal and nonverbal—you send to those around you. How are they similar or different from what you saw and learned growing up? What might you want to change?
- In the next week, keep track of whose voice is in your head or whose actions you're imitating and what the underlying message is. You can do this by keeping a thought journal on your phone, tablet, or a small notepad (choose something that you carry around with you). Anytime the message or behavior occurs, write it down in your journal. At the end of each day, review your thought journal, paying specific attention to the frequency, timing, and content of the message or behavior. Having an increased awareness of some of the messages you've internalized and behaviors you've emulated is the first step in the change process.
- What alternative message or behavior do you want to embody? In

other words, what do you want your new mantra to be? For example, "I am enough," "God loves me," "I am working hard," "He is with me," or even simply, "I am okay." Ground yourself in these messages by randomly reminding yourself of this throughout the day. Use it as a password, or set reminders in your calendar.

- When you find yourself acting or thinking according to past, potentially negative messages, replace those thoughts with your alternative, stabilizing message.

Chapter Three

Mirror, Mirror, on the Wall

Picture this: You're at a party in a crowded room with a lot of activity around you. You notice a guy across the way. He's talking with a group of other people but facing you. You're talking to your girlfriend but can also see him. You try to slyly take interest, hoping your eyes will meet. You vaguely remember hearing about the yawn test, or as I like to call it, the if-I-see-a-cute-guy-across-the-way-and-want-to-know-if-he's-noticed-me-at-all-I-will-purposely-yawn-and-then-watch-out-of-the-corner-of-my-eye-to-see-if-he-yawns-too theory! So you go for it; you make yourself yawn. Then you watch and wait for a second or two. (Cue the *Jeopardy!* jingle here.) He yawns. Sweet! You're in luck. You deftly make your way to his side of the room, thanking your mirror neurons with each step.

Mirror Neurons: He Notices Me, He Notices Me Not

Cutting-edge research in neuroscience reveals that *mirror neurons* are the physiological basis for social interactions and social learning theory. In the 1990s, neuroscientists discovered these mirror neurons while studying macaque monkeys that were implanted with electrodes to track individual neurons.[1] (In case you don't remember from biology class, neurons are cells that carry messages between our brain and the rest of our body.) When the monkey ate a peanut, a specific electrode fired. But that same neuron fired when the monkey *watched* one of the scientists eat a peanut. It was as if the monkey himself had eaten the peanut! In other words, the researchers discovered that the monkey's brain became active just by watching the actions of another. Thus, the base definition for mirror neurons are neurons that fire when we observe an action performed by another; the neuron "mirrors" the behavior of the other, almost as if the observer were acting.

Studies about the role of mirror neurons in humans are ongoing, but at the simplest level they explain the yawn test and the impetus behind some of our unconscious behaviors, specifically our ability to be empathetic. As humans we have the capability—wired in our brains—to mirror the behavioral intentions and emotional states of others. Think about when you last approached a group of friends who were laughing. What was your response? Most likely you started to smile or giggle before you even heard the reason why they were laughing. Mirror neurons prime us to mimic *and* to like those who mimic us. One fascinating study found that unconscious mimicry is deeply social; we are more likely to mimic someone from the same ethnic group but less likely to imitate a stigmatized person who is obese or from a group we view with prejudice. Even more so, we don't like it when we are mimicked by someone from an "out group."[2]

*✦ ✦ We are relational beings, born with a social brain
    hardwired for connection.*

What does this mean? Why are mirror neurons making such a big splash today? One of the primary reasons this new research captivates us is because it confirms what we have known since the beginning of time— we are relational beings, born with a *social* brain hardwired for connection. Now, thanks to brain imagery and other advanced technologies, we can see what is going on in the brain during relational interactions.

When we examine our brain while in relationships, we see that from birth the brain begins taking in signals from our social environment. Research indicates that a baby whose parent responds sympathetically and in sync to its emotional cues tends to express more pleasure, is more interested in exploration, and is easier to calm down. An unresponsive parent, on the other hand, often prompts an infant to exhibit a sad or even angry face, crying and fussing, "pick me up" gestures, and a more apathetic, listless body.[3] Parents who respond angrily or impatiently reinforce the baby's quick rise to distress. This research illustrates the clear connection between external social signals and our internal, emotional world.

Scientist and clinician Daniel Siegel speaks of this connection as *interpersonal integration*. The very essence of our brain is social, and it is made to relate with the brain of each person we interact with. What happens *between* brains has a great deal of impact on what happens *within* each of our individual brains.[4] Said another way, "me" and "you" are fundamentally interrelated, as our very sense of self is constructed by interactions with others. Interpersonal integration is the "me" that discovers meaning by belonging to a "we." Although as a culture we celebrate individualism, our brain structure requires interdependence and we thrive in relationship with others.

It is not hard to see how the realities of mirror neurons and interpersonal integration map onto our Christian faith. First and foremost, God is an inherently relational and personal being. He is three in one, after all—Father, Son, and Holy Spirit. The Bible affirms the existence of three distinct persons identified as one God of the universe. It is not merely the triune God that confirms God's relational being but also the way that the three persons of the Godhead personally relate to and fellowship with each other. The Father is fundamentally interrelated to the Son, who is interrelated to the Spirit.

Another way to think about interpersonal integration is this: I discover who I am by belonging to another. Our very sense of self is shaped by our relational experience. Talk about the power of relationships!

Emotional Development: She Loves Me, She Loves Me Not

Mirror neurons, then, underscore the importance of our early experiences within our families and their impact on how we respond to and interact within all relationships throughout life. Developmental researchers, physicians, and educators alike are interested in the effects of our home environment on our capability, especially our cognitive functioning and intelligence quotient, yet our emotional quotient (EQ) is often given a backseat. If you're reading this and don't even know what EQ is, you're not alone. EQ measures our ability to understand and regulate our own emotions as well as read and understand the emotions of others. Emotions are central in our endeavors—from cognitive processing to social behavior and even to physical health.

Think over your day so far and specifically the way you felt after having a conversation with a close friend, parent, coworker, or significant other. That event—talking with your friend—triggers an emotional response because you care about the outcome. If you felt happy, you were all in. Sad? You withdrew. If you were frightened, you moved away. And if you were angry, you geared up to fight.

✦ *Emotions are rapid appraisals of a situation that prepare us for action.*

At a base level, emotions are rapid appraisals of a situation that prepare us for action; they arise from ongoing exchanges between people and their environment, and they serve different functions as circumstances and social surroundings change.[5] Emotions affect the way we relate to our environment and serve as our barometer. Understanding our emotional development helps us as we engage in intimate relationships. Let's quickly take a look at their origins—whether emotions are learned or innate and if they can be trusted.

Basic emotions, such as happiness, sadness, fear, interest, surprise, anger, and disgust are universal in humans, and mothers of one-month-old babies already report being able to differentiate these emotions.[6] Over time, as our central nervous system develops and we engage in relationships, our emotions become clearer, more organized signals (or at least that is the hope!).

It is not until eighteen to twenty-four months, when infants are developing a sense of being separate, unique individuals, that self-conscious emotions such as shame, guilt, embarrassment, and pride emerge. There's a key difference, however, between basic emotions and self-conscious emotions. And that is *adult input*. Depending on the culture one is raised in, adults provide instruction in *when* to feel ashamed, proud, or guilty. For many of us Americans, we were taught to feel pride in personal achievement—whether that's running the fastest, winning a game, or getting good grades—and shame in failure, such as losing a competition, failing an exam, or messing up an opportunity.

Guess what else emerges during this second year of life? *Self-concept*, or our sense of self. As two-year-olds, we must simultaneously navigate both self-conscious emotions and the development of our identity! It shouldn't come as a surprise, then, that toddlers become increasingly sensitive to praise and criticism (or what might be blame and shame in some families). The implication is that feedback from significant adults takes on greater importance in a toddler's eyes by age three. Self-conscious emotions are clearly linked to self-evaluation.

As you can imagine, the quality of the adult feedback we receive as children influences our self-evaluation. If your parents frequently comment on your overall *performance* and *worth*—regardless of whether it's positive or negative ("What a pathetic job," "Good girl," "You're so smart/pretty/artistic/athletic")—you tend to experience self-conscious emotions more intensely. There is more shame after failure and more pride after success. When parents focus on effort or a specific aspect of performance ("You studied really hard for that test, and it shows. Nice work!"), however, we not only have more appropriate levels of shame and pride but also greater persistence on difficult tasks.[7]

Getting to the Heart of It

The influence that parents have on our emotions and behaviors relates to the work of Carol Dweck, a psychologist from Stanford University who has studied the concept of mindset. Dweck has identified two ways of viewing and approaching life—with a *fixed mindset* or with a *growth mindset*. She purports that the mindset you adopt for yourself profoundly affects the way you live your life. Those with a fixed mindset believe their abilities and qualities are carved in stone; they are unchangeable, so you better hope you've got a good amount of intelligence, charisma, and moral character! Those with the growth mindset, however, believe that their basic qualities are cultivated through effort and perseverance.

Intelligence, talent, and personality can change and grow through effort and experience.[8]

For a quick measure of your mindset, which of the following statements from Dweck's *Mindset* do you agree with?

- Intelligence is something very basic about you that you can't change very much.
- You can learn new things, but you can't really change how intelligent you are.
- No matter how much intelligence you have, you can always change it quite a bit.
- You can always substantially change how intelligent you are.[9]

If you found yourself gravitating more toward the first and second statement, you tend to be more of a fixed mindset person. If the third and fourth statement resonated with you, you are more growth-minded.

★ *What does mindset have to do with our early experiences or the health of later relationships?*

But what does mindset have to do with our early experiences or the health of later relationships? A lot! Think about the messages you received as a child from your parents as it related to your personality, intelligence, and ability. Here are some potential examples:

- "You're so smart; straight As without even studying!"
- "You're a natural athlete; you're the fastest on the team, and you don't even have to practice!"
- "Oh boy—you are quick and good! Look how speedy you were in doing these problems . . . and you didn't even make one mistake. Brilliant!"
- "That's perfect! You're perfect."
- "You're so handsome/beautiful."
- "Look at that drawing; you're going to be an amazing artist!"
- "You are a natural at piano."

At first glance, I imagine most of you are thinking, *These are great—positive and uplifting. Who wouldn't want to hear that?* A lot of them might even sound familiar to you; perhaps you have others to add to the list. How, you might wonder, could these messages—overflowing with praise and adoration—impact our self-conscious emotions such as pride, shame, or guilt, and our actual motivation and performance?

First, let's consider the messages behind the message. While parents typically make such statements with the intention of building up and praising their children, often we internalize a second message, one that lies beneath the spoken words. For the preceding statements, you might hear the following behind your parents' spoken words:

- "If I have to study, I'm not as smart as I thought I was."
- "If I'm no longer the fastest, I'm not a good athlete."
- "If I can't quickly solve a problem, I'm not very capable."
- "If I'm not perfect, I'm not worth it."
- "If someone else is 'the beauty,' I guess I'm not beautiful."
- "If I try to draw a more complicated picture and mess up, they'll see I'm not an artist."
- "If I have to practice hard at piano, I'm a disappointment to others."

All of these are potentially accompanied by intense shame and guilt in the face of failure and inflated pride in the face of success.

In other words, these fixed mindset messages make us more vulnerable as children (and adults!) to insecurities and low self-esteem. The stakes are higher if we mess up, and so is the shame. And so, to protect ourselves, we learn to play it safe—not taking on any new challenges for fear of failure. Although we might boast about being the smartest, fastest, and best, underneath is a lurking insecurity. *What if I make a mistake—what will they think of me? What if a problem is hard and I can't do it, what does that mean?* Dweck's research indicates that children who receive fixed mindset messages doubt themselves, avoid challenges, give up easily when the going gets tough, and are crushed by mistakes.

Messages that are more specific and focus on effort, observable behavior, and performance (as opposed to outcome), on the other hand, tend to cultivate a growth mindset. Maybe you heard messages like these when you were growing up:

- "You worked really diligently on your science project—I'm glad you learned so much about photosynthesis."
- "You've got talent as a runner; keep practicing and working hard, and you'll most likely continue to be fast."
- "Oh, you completed those problems quickly without making one mistake. Seems like you need more of a challenge!"
- "I appreciate the use of color in your drawing; the way you used the purple and blue together really stands out."
- "I so enjoy hearing you play piano; I can tell you have worked hard at that song. It sounds wonderful!"

When we are encouraged to work hard, embrace mistakes, and face challenges as an opportunity to learn—we do just that. We also tend to have more fun in the process!

✦ *The feedback we received from our parents in our
    early years sends a message and impacts our sense
    of self-worth.*

Bottom line: the feedback we received from our parents in our early years sends a message and impacts our sense of self-worth. From verbal messages to nonverbal messages (think mirror neurons!), our brain is being shaped by our experiences. What our parents mirror back to us helps us construct our emotional lives—and our sense of identity and self-worth has a huge impact on how we behave in later, intimate relationships. Can you see why your "once upon a time" is so incredibly important?

★ ★ ★

"Even though my parents always told me, 'You can do anything you put your mind to,' I figured that must not be true because my mom always did things for me. So I just thought I was incapable. And I stopped trying."

Twenty-four-year-old Amber was matter-of-fact as she shared this in one of our last sessions together. She was getting ready to move away from her hometown for the first time, counting down the days until she hopped on the plane and flew across the country to attend a photography institute. I wasn't sure what she was more excited for: starting over in a new city or ending what felt like very-small-town life.

"Your parents' well-intended words didn't match their actions, eh?"

"Not at all," she responded emphatically.

"And so you just figured you must not be competent. Or maybe you thought that if you *did* try something—if you really put your mind to something initially—and you didn't get it immediately, well, then you were a failure."

Amber reflected for a moment on my words and then let out a long sigh. "Maybe that's why I give up so easily when I can't figure things out right away. This whole job search is a perfect example."

Bull's-eye, I thought to myself excitedly as I nonchalantly inquired, "How so?"

"Well, I can't help but wonder if photography school is simply a way for me to postpone the inevitable. I mean, my parents are fully paying for me to go to New York, and it is something I am excited about. But is it really my own? I worry that it's just . . ." She let out an exasperated groan.

"Go on," I said, gently but assertively.

Her tone changed from frustrated to reflective. "I don't know what to do with myself. And to be honest, I don't really want to work hard at a job. Heck, I don't even know how to go about getting a job, and so I just give up before I begin. I give up in my own head. I don't push myself. I am afraid of failure. And if something doesn't happen right away, then forget it."

Tears formed in her eyes. "I do that with dating too. Right?"

"Give up if it doesn't work out right away, or if it's hard, you mean?" I clarified.

She nodded.

"What do you think?" I asked.

"Let's see. With Chase, there wasn't really chemistry. Matt just annoyed me. And Troy . . . Ah, Troy—it just didn't seem like the timing was right with me heading off to New York. It would be too much work to date long-distance."

There was a long pause.

"Amber, it seems like you are making a connection between your mindset—your fear of failure and perceived inability—and the decisions you make. Whether it's a decision about a guy, job, career path, or move, you worry that it might be hard—too much work—and you might not be successful right away, so you quit before you start. Because that's the safest choice."

Amber nodded. "I'm so used to my mom doing things for me—rescuing me, really—that I don't know how to persevere. I give up way too easily. Even with guys. When things don't work out right away, I don't bother."

"If there's not chemistry from the get-go—then it must not be right," I said, quoting her own words from our previous conversation.

"Yeah, with Chase, I figured that. As you know."

"Yes, I know. And Troy?" I asked.

Amber's shoulders sank as she sighed deeply. And then a look of disgust came over her face as she said, "Oh no. I realize I was waiting for my mom to rescue me . . . to tell me how to break up with Troy—what to say to him and how to communicate that the distance wasn't going to work out."

Self-Efficacy: I Love Me, I Love Me Not

Self-efficacy is the belief in one's capabilities to accomplish a task or succeed in a situation. Albert Bandura (of the previously mentioned "monkey see, monkey do" research) defined it in 1977 as part of his social cognitive theory, purporting that our sense of self-efficacy plays a major role in how we approach challenges, goals, and tasks. According to Bandura, people with high self-efficacy—those who believe they can perform well—are more likely to approach challenges as something to be overcome and mastered rather than avoided.

Sound familiar? Like mindset, self-efficacy is developed through our external experiences; it also takes into account our self-perception. So it is through our experiences—past accomplishments, constructive feedback and encouragement, observational learning—and our self-concept that we begin to internalize a sense of "I can do this; I am capable."

In Amber's case, she never had a chance to call an accomplishment her own. She never learned to work hard, to overcome a challenge, or to learn from a mistake—resulting in her belief that she must not be capable.

It is through our experiences . . . and our self-concept that we begin to internalize a sense of "I can do this; I am capable."

When I was a child, my mom thought I hung the moon. It's not that I thought I could do no wrong, but rather I grew up with a deep sense of knowing I was loved immensely. I can remember the look of fondness and joy in my mom's eyes when she watched me—whether I was "performing" some sort of silly song and dance or dozing off to sleep, I knew I was special and loved. And I believed it; I believed I was worthy of someone else's love and attention.

The self-discovery that occurs in our early years continues with us as we journey through life. Perhaps it's no surprise, then, that confidence arose within me as I grew. I felt worthy and capable, and knew that even when I messed up, I was still loved deeply. Undoubtedly, one of the greatest gifts we can receive is just that—knowing we are loved by another, no matter what. As a believer, what an incredible gift it is to know that I am loved by the Creator and King of the universe. Yes, Jesus loves me.

This sense of being unconditionally loved is especially necessary in our earliest days, months, and years. As infants, our sense of self and identity—and our basic emotional state—is reflected back to us via our parents' eyes. We look to them to mirror our worth and help regulate our emotions. And so, depending on what is reflected back, our vision of ourselves develops.

When we believe in someone else, we make them capable of what they are becoming. What a gift, then, my mom gave me—she believed in me. And *I* knew she believed in me; I felt it. So I believed in me.

I developed self-efficacy. Thanks to the ways in which I was cared for—both when I succeeded and when I failed—I knew that I was capable.

Self-confidence sprang up as a result and has grounded me throughout my journey. So when "ring by spring" was rampant my senior year of college, I remained confident. When I was a bridesmaid eight times (yes, eight!) and never a bride, I knew I was going to be okay. When I turned thirty and was single, I did not question my self-worth. I could approach both singleness and dating relationships with assurance—grounded in the knowledge that I was valuable, lovable, and capable, no matter what.

What about you? What was mirrored back to you in your formative years and what were the messages you were given? In other words—what do you believe about yourself? Moreover, how do these beliefs affect the way you approach and maintain intimate relationships? It is hard—if not impossible—to receive love if we don't believe ourselves to be lovable.

If you find yourself struggling with self-confidence and embracing a fixed mindset, know you are not alone and take heart—these things are malleable! You will, however, need to actively and intentionally work toward emotional and relational health, and as previously mentioned, the first step is awareness. Engage in realistic self-assessment about your current mindset and efficacy, and if desired, acknowledge and explore ways in which this was a blind spot in your family of origin. Often the best place to work through these emotions, without engaging in the blame game, is in the safety of a counselor's office. Successful resolution means believing you are loved, worthy, and capable of change and growth!

It's worth mentioning that although your parents raised you with the best of intentions, they are human—like all of us—and may have failed you in certain ways. It is healthy to name their shortcomings and allow yourself the freedom to experience the accompanying emotions of anger and sadness. If they claim responsibility for these blind spots, healing is easier.

Research indicates that when we have higher self-efficacy—when we believe in our own capabilities—we are more likely to successfully negotiate and resolve relationship conflict, interact with our partner in an optimistic and uncritical manner, share responsibility within the relationship, communicate more openly, and be more satisfied in the relationship.[10] Think about it—if you believe that you are competent and valuable, that what you say and do makes a difference, then you are not going to be crushed when you don't get asked out on a second date, passive when it comes to dating and marriage, or avoidant when challenges arise and the going gets tough in your relationship. Instead, you will exert more effort when needed, persist longer in the face of difficulty, and work hard for yourself and your partner, knowing you make a difference.

> *God Himself . . . created us in His image and then expressed our worth by sending Christ to conquer death on our behalf.*

For Christians who claim the Bible as a love letter from God and believe Christ is in us—the hope of glory—we have the ultimate reason to know our value and to believe in our self-worth and capability. God Himself, the maker of heaven and earth, created us in His image and then expressed our worth by sending Christ to conquer death on our behalf. God declared His love for us—and therefore our worthiness—on the cross. Indeed, we are loved with an everlasting love (Jer. 31:3). May each one of us claim that truth, regardless of the brokenness that is inherent in all our stories.

Summing Up
- The recent discovery of mirror neurons—neurons that fire in our brain when we simply observe another's behavior—reveals that our brain is hardwired to be social.
- The very nature of the triune God is inherently social, and we are image bearers of Christ—created to be in relationship with Him and others.
- In our early days and years, when we are in a relationship with a caregiver who is sympathetic and attuned to our needs, our mirror neurons kick in and we learn to regulate our own emotions.
- We discover our very sense of self by being a part of another; this is known as interpersonal integration. And when we are better integrated, we are more able to emotionally self-regulate.
- Feelings of self-worth and self-efficacy (our ability to accomplish a task) are shaped by our external experiences and what is mirrored back to us.

So What?

The way we feel about ourselves today—our capability, competence, and worth—can be traced back to the way we were treated as children and affects how we approach and maintain intimate relationships.

Our identity began developing when we were about one and a half to two years old and is rooted in the feedback we received from those in our world. The adults who cared for us, and the culture we were raised in, shaped our identity and emotional lives, and even more specifically, our self-worth and self-conscious emotions. The feedback we received as children when we attempted or completed a task shapes our current mindset—the way in which we approach life and its challenges.

When we have a clearer image of our early family dynamic—the ways in which we were attended to, cared for, praised, criticized, doted on, reprimanded, shamed, or exalted—we can better understand the forces that shaped our identity, emotional lives, and mindset, and we can more firmly grasp why we act the way we do in our relationships. And with knowledge comes power. By gaining awareness of our self-perception and actively working to ensure that our self-image is healthy and positive, we can set ourselves up for stronger, more successful relationships that aren't mired in unresolved emotional conflicts from our past.

Now What? Practical Applications

- When you think back over your childhood years, whose love and admiration were you sure of? In other words, who thought you hung the moon (and you knew they thought that)? How did you know it? What did it feel like? Is that person still in your life today, and if so, what is your relationship with them like?
- What was the emotional climate of your home growing up? Were emotions talked about, expressed, avoided, exaggerated, or denied? How did your parents handle their own emotions when you were young?
- Can you remember a time when you felt like you disappointed your parents? Did you feel like that often? If so, how did that affect your self-esteem during your childhood and adolescence?
- What was mirrored back to you as a child regarding your self-worth?

What were the messages, both verbal and nonverbal, you received about your inherent value, worth, and capability?

- If God's love for you was discussed during your childhood, how was it characterized and what were the messages you internalized?
- How do you evaluate yourself today regarding your value and worth? Specifically, do you think of yourself as inherently lovable? If not, recognize the shortcomings of your upbringing and environment as you simultaneously claim your inherent value as a child of God. It might be helpful to do this in the context of professional counseling.
- What mindset messages did you receive as a child or adolescent? When you did something well, what was the response? How about when you made a mistake or failed at something?
- What messages do you espouse today (to yourself and others)?

Chapter Four

It All Goes Back to the Toy Box

They had been married two years and twice she had been unfaithful. "One of the affairs was merely physical," Rebecca was quick to say in our first session. "It really didn't mean much to me, except it made me feel good about myself—my body."

"And the other one . . . this most recent one?" Jack asked, with both anger and sadness in his voice.

She went quiet as she shifted her gaze intently on me. Determination and despair filled her eyes, along with tears. Rebecca remained silent. So did Jack.

From an early age, Rebecca surmised that girls and women were to be pretty, cute, beautiful, and sexy. Boys and men, on the other hand, were to be strong, smart, and adventurous. They were the rescuers, and women were in need of saving. In her mind, all the puzzle pieces fit together: strong and weak, independent and dependent, the hero and the helpless.

"When I was six, my dad left the family in pursuit of another woman and my mom found another man to take care of us. I learned that men were to be the providers and protectors."

"And women were to be . . . ?" I let my sentence trail off.

"The princesses. The beauty of the story," Rebecca was quick to reply.

"And my mom was a real beauty. I can remember watching her fling her long, silky brown hair over her shoulder as she threw her head back and smiled at the new man in her life. It worked every time."

"With Bill and Gary?" I glanced at my notes to find the names of Rebecca's stepdads.

She nodded.

"So you learned that women could use their looks and their bodies to get what they want?" I asked.

She slowly nodded.

Jack, who had been attentively listening, quietly said, "That's how she got me. I was captivated by her physical presence."

"But once we got married, you didn't seem to care as much," Rebecca stated with frustration in her voice.

"What do you mean, I didn't seem to care as much? I cared more!" Jack looked at her with a furrowed brow as he spoke. "But I knew I didn't have to compete with anyone else. You were mine. We were married." Jack paused and his voice softened as he said, "I trusted you."

His earnestness was met with Rebecca's resentment as she quickly responded, "But you didn't pay attention to me."

And then anger filled the room as Jack raised his voice and exclaimed, "So it's my fault now that you've been unfaithful in our marriage? I wasn't paying enough attention to you; that's the reason you've had two affairs?"

"I never said it was your fault," Rebecca retorted. "I said you weren't paying attention to me."

I jumped in just as things were escalating. "When someone pays attention to you, Rebecca, how does that make you feel?"

"Cared for. Loved. Like I matter."

"So if they don't pay attention to you, you question their love. You feel as if you don't matter as much. Perhaps you even question your own self-worth and value?"

Tears filled Rebecca's eyes as she looked at me and nodded.

The Gender Divide: Pink Versus Blue

For the past ten years I have asked college students to anonymously write down the messages they've heard about gender while growing up. I have two folders in my office—one labeled *Gender Messages, Women* and the other *Gender Messages, Men*. Here is a sampling of what's inside:

<u>Gender Messages, Women</u>
- It's important to find a man to take care of me.
- Work out a lot; guys don't like out-of-shape girls.
- The way I dress is important. Looks matter.
- I shouldn't be too assertive.
- Wow, you're actually smart.
- It's okay to cry; sometimes it gets girls what they want.
- Be "nice." Accommodate and please others.
- Men are the leaders.
- You will always be my little princess.
- Don't you want to wear makeup and dresses?

<u>Gender Messages, Men</u>
- Be strong. Don't be a sissy.
- Boys don't cry.
- I should find a pretty woman to marry someday.
- A good job is important, but making money is the most important.
- When I started to enjoy cooking, I was teased. I learned that men aren't supposed to be in the kitchen; that was women's work.
- Men don't talk about what they feel—it shows weakness.
- Boys should be doing sports, not music/art/theater. If you do one of the latter, you're gay.
- Win at all costs.
- Men should take care of women. Take the lead.
- Don't play like a girl.

Like my students, we have all received messages about what it means to be a man or woman. From the moment we are born, we are treated differently depending on our sex.[1] Baby girls are talked to, held, and hugged more than baby boys.[2] In their early years, girls hear twice as many diminutives as boys—"doggie," "blankie," and "paci" as opposed to "dog," "blanket," and "pacifier."[3] As soon as babies can sit up on their own, boys spend more time sitting and playing alone than girls do; girls continue to be held and cuddled.[4] Parents tend to talk about their sons as more intelligent than their daughters.[5] Additionally, parents talk more about emotions and display a wider range of emotions—with the exception of anger—with their daughters than with their sons.[6] Fast-forward a couple of years and research indicates that teachers interact more with boys and call on them more frequently, and when boys call out answers, teachers listen. When girls call out, they are reprimanded for breaking the rules and reminded to follow the rules, be polite, and raise their hands.[7]

> *✦✦✦ The marketing of toys is more gendered today than fifty years ago when gender discrimination was the norm.*

Outside of the home and classroom, we are also bombarded with gendered messages and images. Onesies read "Smart like Daddy" for boys and "Pretty like Mommy" for girls. T-shirts marketed to young girls read, "I'm too pretty to do my homework so my brother has to do it for me," and the original Teen Talk Barbie said, "Math class is tough." The marketing of toys is more gendered today than fifty years ago when gender discrimination was the norm; for example, Disney's website store has explicit toy categories "for boys" and "for girls."[8] Seas of pink cookery sets and beauty-related products are separated from cars, spaceships, science sets, and all things adventure. Cartoons, movies, and books also depict this gender divide—male characters are portrayed as more competent, confident, and courageous than their emotional, passive, and tentative female counterparts.

This tale of gender difference and divide is woven deeply into the fabric of contemporary childhood. Young girls today grow up with the message that they can be anything—as long as it's beauty-focused, passive, and pretty. Perhaps it's no surprise, then, that girls as young as six years old attribute brilliance to the male gender.[9] Boys today learn at a young age to be strong, independent, smart, and unemotional. Most distressing, research indicates that girls and boys begin to *act* on these internalized beliefs in childhood, and these thoughts and behaviors are then carried into adulthood. Girls grow up to be women who are tentative in their language, hesitant to take the lead, dependent, anxious, doubtful of their abilities, and affected with body image issues and eating disorders. On the other hand, boys who swallow this gender stereotype grow up to be men who are afraid of failure, ashamed of weakness, more aggressive, misogynistic, and suicidal.

> *When we see our partner as . . . "the one who doesn't understand because he or she is not like me," it is detrimental to building healthy relationships.*

Pitting boys against girls, men against women, places a constraint on both sexes and pigeonholes both men and women. It leads to a self-fulfilling prophecy—the more we believe something is true, the more likely we are to act in a way that makes it true. If men continue to hear the message that they are poor communicators, they eventually internalize that and stop trying to communicate effectively. If we believe in these "innate" sex-based traits, we often end the conversation with our opposite-sex partner prematurely, concluding, "She or he just doesn't get it." In turn, women are taught that they are overemotional and irrational and not cut out for leadership, so they shy away from taking a stand. The cost of believing in these radical gender differences is huge—for all of us. When we see our partner as "the other" or "the one who doesn't understand because he or she is not like me," it is detrimental to building healthy relationships, families, and communities.

It's a Purple World

What does the *actual research* show about gender differences? For the first twelve months of life, there is absolutely no difference between babies in color or toy preference. In fact, both girls and boys at twelve months prefer dolls over cars and reddish colors over blue.[10] Then something changes for these little ones as they enter toddlerhood—they absorb familial and cultural messages of what it means to be a boy or a girl. Whether whispered or shouted, the messages are clear: Boys are to like blue instead of pink and trucks instead of dolls, and they should be strong and smart. Girls are to like all things pink and pretty, and they should be gentle and cute. Children as young as two years old categorize themselves as boys or girls, begin to build a cognitive framework of what that means, and start acting and behaving accordingly. By age four, they are convinced that certain toys are appropriate for one gender but not the other. And so it goes. In junior high, girls with the highest math competency have the lowest self-esteem, and by college, girls rate their mathematical abilities significantly lower than boys even though there is no observable difference between the two genders.[11] Children learn at an early age not only to apply these gender attributes to themselves and others but also to evaluate their own adequacy as persons based on whether they meet these expectations.

In "The Gender Similarities Hypothesis," researcher Janet Shibley Hyde conducted a meta-analysis of hundreds of scientific studies about gender difference. Her conclusion? Seventy-eight percent of stereotypical gender differences are small or close to zero, and there are as many differences within the sex as there are between sexes.[12] Let me say that again: there are as many differences among men as there are between men and women. In other words, a man might be more similar to a woman than he is to another man. This is known as the gender similarities hypothesis. Instead of claiming that men are from Mars and women are from Venus, it boldly states that we are all from planet Earth.

Think about it in your own life. If you are a woman, can you think of a man you have more things in common with than another woman? Or if you are a man, is there a woman who you find yourself more similar to than another man? I imagine so. We are all human beings, equally endowed with a sense of agency and consciousness, regardless of our gender.

"So God created mankind in his own image, in the image of God he created them; male and female he created them" (Gen. 1:27). *Both* men and women are relational beings created in the image of God. Nowhere in the Bible do we see that women are to be passive, emotional, and demure, nor is there any biblical passage that says men are to be uncommunicative, adventurous, and independent. As New Testament scholar Philip Payne states, "Scripture's affirmations of the equality of men and women and its affirmation of women called by God to exercise authority alongside or over men are so clear and numerous. . . . Biblical evidence for the equal standing of men and women in the life of the church is inescapable."[13]

★ *Nowhere in the Bible do we see that women are to be passive, emotional, and demure, nor is there any biblical passage that says men are to be uncommunicative, adventurous, and independent.*

To cultivate more intimate connections, we must break free of suffocating and limiting gender stereotypes. This means challenging gender-based expectations and assumptions that might pigeonhole you and your partner. If, for example, your significant other excels in baking or bill paying, their gender should not dictate assumed roles. By celebrating our unique personhood, we experience harmony and joy and work harder to resolve conflict.

★ ★ ★

Rebecca had wholeheartedly bought into the idea that women were to use their beauty and sex appeal to get what they want. In her case, she wanted attention, love, and care. When she received these, her worth as a person was validated. She was valuable when men—the stronger and more powerful sex—paid attention to her. For most of her young adult life, she successfully used her looks and her body to command attention and power, but when she and Jack settled in to marriage, things fell apart.

"You stopped pursuing me," Rebecca told Jack. "When we were dating, I knew you wanted to be with me. It was clear from the way you looked at me, pursued me, and paid attention to me, especially if we were out together at a party or event."

"Right. I wanted other men to know you were mine. My girlfriend," Jack responded.

"Well, don't you want other men to know that I'm your wife?"

"Yes, but it's different now that we're married. I trust that we're committed to each other . . . that I don't have to prove my love to you. That you know I think you're beautiful—not just on the outside. I love you for who you are as a person."

Rebecca's face softened and her eyes moistened. "I don't really know . . ." Her words trailed off as she began to cry.

"Know what, Rebecca?" I gently inquired.

Tears streamed down her face as she shook her head and muttered, "Never mind."

"You don't really know that Jack loves you?" I wasn't going to let it go.

She shook her head. And then in between sobs she said, "I don't really know who I am as a person."

Silence and insight filled the room. I broke it minutes later by quietly repeating Rebecca's words: "You don't know who you are as a person." And then I continued. "But you know who you are *supposed* to be?"

She nodded, wiped her tears, and then rather assertively said, "Oh yes. I know *exactly* who I am supposed to be. I am supposed to be a nice little girl—princess, I mean—who looks pretty, stays in shape, doesn't eat too much, is kind, pleases others, doesn't talk too much, and waits around for my prince to come. What happens after that—clearly, as we all can see from my behavior—I don't know. The fairy tale comes to a screeching halt."

Only when we . . . ground our self-worth in our inherent, God-given value can we thrive both in and out of relationships.

We had our work cut out for us—a majority of it around challenging the deeply held but erroneous belief that Rebecca was to be captivating in order to be worthy and beautiful in order to be loved. Her internalized ideas of gender, and all the "shoulds" that accompanied her role as a woman, needed to be reset. From seemingly benign greetings exchanged between other women ("Cute purse," "Great outfit," "I love your hair") to more deeply held stereotypes about gender and power, Rebecca began to see the implications of her gender-divided thinking. Over time, she developed a new understanding of her self-worth and role in her marriage—one of *mutual* dependence, autonomy, brokenness, and healing. Only when we identify and correct misguided—but ubiquitous—gender stereotypes and relationship roles and ground our self-worth in our inherent, God-given value can we thrive both in and out of relationships.

Summing Up
- From the moment we enter this world, we begin receiving implicit and explicit messages that relate to our gender. Girls are socialized to be dependent and emotionally expressive whereas boys receive the message that they are to be independent and unemotional.
- The tale of gender difference and divide negatively impacts our relationships and pigeonholes boys and girls, men and women.
- Psychological research speaks to the gender similarities hypothesis, stating that there are as many differences *within* a sex as there are *between* the sexes.
- Both women and men were created in the image of God to be equals.

So What?
The way we conceptualize and view our roles as women and men—how similar or dissimilar we are from those of the opposite sex—greatly impacts the choices we make in our relationships and in our lives in general.

We begin receiving messages—from our families, communities, and culture—about what it means to be male or female in our earliest days of life. When we believe there are innate character differences between the sexes, we narrow our view of ourselves and of the opposite sex. This constricted view impacts the way we think, feel, and act in our friendships, workplace, and intimate relationships. Specifically in intimate relationships, when we see our partner as "the other" who "just doesn't get it," we give up more easily on opportunities of knowing and being known.

When we are aware of the truth—that men and women have more similarities than differences—we set ourselves and our partner free from gender stereotypes to be valued for who we truly are. We work harder to understand differences and resolve conflicts in our intimate relationships, knowing there is nothing in the other that is completely foreign to us—resulting in more intimate and caring connections with each other, based on mutual respect and dependence.

Now What? Practical Applications

- What were the messages you received as a child regarding your gender? Think through what was both said and modeled by your family, church, school, mentors, and community.
- If you had a sibling of the opposite sex, what messages did they receive? How were those messages the same or different from yours?
- What did you learn about femininity and masculinity from books, television shows, music, stories, and movies?
- In what ways was the church a socializing agent in your conception of gender?
- What do you believe today about boys and girls, men and women, regarding similarities and differences? Are there certain "shoulds" that you hold yourself and others of the same sex to? What are your expectations for those of the opposite sex?
- How have you acted on your idea of what it means to be male or female? In other words, have you behaved in a way that didn't feel like you because of a gender stereotype? If so, call it out for what it is—limiting and divisive—and begin embracing your unique voice!
- Consider and discuss areas of friction in your relationships that might have their source in gender-based expectations. Talk with your partner about gender messages they received—both blatant and subtle—and how they feel about them.
- Track the interactions you have with men and women, girls and boys, over the next couple of days—this ranges from the way you greet each other (what words you use), to the focus and topics of conversations, to your internal thoughts and feelings about the other. What do you notice? Is there a difference in the way you think about and treat men and women?

PART TWO

Deconstructing the Myths of Love

CHAPTER FIVE

Anchoring in Rough Seas

As a sophomore in college, Sarah began counseling because of increasing levels of anxiety, particularly surrounding decision-making in life and relationships. Should she major in biology or chemistry, spend a summer working in her hometown or abroad, live off campus or on? Who would her next roommate be? Did her friend, Dan, want to pursue romance or was she misreading the signals? Sarah was angst-ridden and overwhelmed by the choices she faced.

As she learned strategies for managing her anxiety, I learned more about the environment in which she grew up. Sarah was raised in a wealthy suburb of Los Angeles and had "everything a girl could want—loving parents, a sweet younger sister, and a solid group of friends." An above-average student, intent in her pursuit of the piano, and generally well adjusted—life was relatively easy. "I was never a party girl but had plenty of friends. One of our favorite Friday night activities was to watch chick flicks like *Mean Girls*, *The Notebook*, and *Crazy, Stupid, Love*. We loved plotting our future lives—envisioning a super fun college experience, the perfect boyfriend, a successful career, and ultimately a beautiful home—kids and dog included." Sarah paused and swallowed hard. "What a joke! I'm so far from any of that and hate the way it makes me feel."

Through our work together, it became clear Sarah's expectations weren't being realized—and certainly not within the time frame she anticipated. Nearing the end of her senior year she had no clear career path, no romantic prospects, and a growing sense of anxiety. By comparing herself to peers, she felt like a failure. "Three of my friends are in a serious relationship—one is engaged. My roommate has been accepted to graduate school—and here I am still wondering if I've chosen the right major. And if one more person asks me what I'll be doing after graduation . . . I'm going to blow!"

★ We all struggle with transition and change.

Sarah was at an exciting crossroads. But, like many young adults, she grappled with the challenges of transitioning into adulthood, accompanied by disappointment and unmet expectations. She is not alone. We all struggle with transition and change. However, brain development, delayed adulthood, a hypersexual culture with romantic expectations scripted by Hollywood, and obsessive reliance on social media makes this season of life especially taxing. In this chapter, we will examine how these disparate but interrelated topics make embracing genuine intimacy and love more difficult and contribute to myths about romance. In subsequent chapters we will consider some of those more widely held myths.

The Hijacked Brain

Brain research over the past twenty-five years has revealed that there are more changes in our brains—specifically our prefrontal cortex—during adolescence and early adulthood than we once thought. The prefrontal cortex, often thought of as the chief *executive* officer or thinking brain, is where rational decision-making resides; it's responsible for things such as working memory, planning, and regulating our moods. It is during our teenage and early twentysomething years that our prefrontal cortex is evolving into its adult shape. Similar to infancy, this period of neurological development is marked by neurons rearranging themselves; they either connect with a buddy (known as neuronal connection) or die off (known as pruning).

There's a caveat, though. We all have a competing chief. It's the chief *emotional* officer, known as the amygdala. The amygdala is the storehouse of all feelings, affections, and passions, and as one of the most highly connected regions of the brain, it "occupies a position at the very geometric center."[1] Without our amygdala, life would have no personal meaning—no passion, excitement, and fun! Because the prefrontal cortex is undergoing change and not fully developed in early adulthood, the amygdala arguably has an upper hand in this competition. Recent discoveries in neuroscience reveal this truth: we rely most heavily on our amygdala during adolescence and early adulthood. Furthermore, our prefrontal cortex—our thinking brain—is not fully developed until age twenty-five. That means that our emotional maturity, self-image, and judgment are not fine-tuned until we are twenty-five years old. Twenty. Five.

Regardless of our age, we all know what it's like to be overcome by emotions. Think of the last time you felt hurt by someone you're close to. What happened? What was your reaction? Did you raise your voice, storm off, go silent, cry, throw something, or say something extreme? Maybe you called it off, broke up, or drove away. Whatever specific reaction you had, I imagine it involved strong emotions. We call this the "amygdala hijack"—when the emotional part of our brain overpowers our rational brain. It literally takes over and we lose rationality. Our anger, hurt, and disappointment consume us.

Shifting Milestones

In addition to research regarding our changing brain and the amygdala hijack, brain scans are also showing that we are better equipped to make major life decisions in our *late* twenties. And those in their late twenties agree! When eighteen to twenty-nine-year-olds were surveyed, only half of them reported feeling like they'd reached adulthood—and the majority of those were in their late twenties.[2]

Perhaps this is why we're seeing a shift in adulthood responsibilities today. More and more twentysomethings are still in school, single, and without kids. Careers, marriage, and parenting are being postponed as young adults explore their own identity and decide what they want out of work, love, and life. Contrary to what many might think, postponing the inevitable—adulthood—and the accompanying tasks associated with it might not be such a bad thing. At least in our early twenties. In light of our changing, not fully developed brain, one could argue it's an adaptive response.

⋆⋆⋆ *Contrary to what many might think, postponing . . . adulthood . . . might not be such a bad thing.*

Given this demographic trend, the field of developmental psychology has acknowledged a new stage of development, known as *emerging adulthood*, which encompasses the years from eighteen to twenty-five. It is a time of seismic change. We're no longer a dependent adolescent but not quite a responsible adult. Opportunities seem endless and many directions are possible; nothing is quite set in stone. Emerging adults explore ideas for work, love, and worldview, without the necessity of committing to any one of them. The scope of independent exploration and volition during emerging adulthood is arguably greater than any other period of life. The world is our oyster: What are we going to do with it?

Sexualization in a #MeToo World

Add technology and popular culture to the mix and we're in a hot mess. More than ever before, children, adolescents, and young adults are being bombarded and inundated with an onslaught of overly sexualized messages about identity and worth. Pornography, a multibillion-dollar industry, is only a click away. Subtler, and yet equally powerful, are teenage stars marketed as sex symbols, models with perfectly toned and tanned bodies, scantily clad Bratz and Barbie dolls, and sexually suggestive advertisements.

The American Psychological Association (APA) formed a task force to examine ways in which girls and women were being sexualized in our culture. They proposed that sexualization occurs when

- a person's value comes only from his or her sexual appeal or behavior, to the exclusion of other characteristics;
- a person is held to a standard that equates physical attractiveness (narrowly defined) with being sexy;
- a person is sexually objectified—that is, made into a thing for others'

sexual use, rather than seen as a person with the capacity for independent action and decision making; and/or
* sexuality is inappropriately imposed upon a person.[3]

Any one of these conditions, according to APA, is an indication of sexualization. In our culture today, we often see all four of these occurring—
short T-shirts that say "Flirt" made for five-year-olds, magazines for pread-
olescent girls giving instructions on how to look sexy and get a boyfriend
by losing ten pounds and straightening their hair, or advertisements that
portray women as little girls with pigtails in adult sexual poses. The harsh
truth is this: countless studies give evidence to the sobering reality of
sexualization. Is it any wonder that today's headlines are filled with allega-
tions and investigations into the sexual misconduct and abuse of women
by men in power, once revered as leaders in their field?

✦✦✦ *Research . . . clearly links sexualization with three*
of the most common mental health issues in girls
and women—eating disorders, depression, and low
self-esteem.

The effects are devastating, for all of us. For women, body image and
comparisons to cultural ideals disrupts thinking; girls and women are less
likely to engage in logical reasoning, mathematical problem-solving, and
spatial skills when they think about their bodies.[4] Self-objectification also
limits the effectiveness of girls' motor performance and physical move-
ment; one study found that girls don't throw as far or use their whole bodies to throw when they are concerned about appearance.[5] Sexualization
undermines confidence and comfort in one's own body, leading girls and
women to feel more shame, anxiety, and self-dissatisfaction. Perhaps the
most troubling of all is the research that clearly links sexualization with
three of the most common mental health issues in girls and women—
eating disorders, depression, and low self-esteem.[6]

Boys and men don't get off the hook easily either. With increased exposure to narrow ideals of female attractiveness, it is more difficult for men
to find an "acceptable" partner or to enjoy being intimate with a woman.

Additionally, the APA reported that when girls and women are seen solely as sexual beings, boys and men often have difficulty relating to them on any other level.[7]

Sexualization and objectification are problematic at any age, but youth and young adults are particularly at risk. Faced with the challenge of developing a cohesive identity, and not yet having the emotional sophistication or cognitive capability to critically analyze sexual messages (remember the competition between the prefrontal cortex and amygdala), young people are the most vulnerable to these inappropriate messages. The more sexual content children and adolescents are exposed to, the more likely they are to have sex at a younger age and engage in high-risk sex—from unprotected and frequent sex to sex with multiple partners and sex accompanied by drug or alcohol use.[8]

An Impossible Script

Hollywood has cornered the market on skewed ideals of romance. On-screen relationships are not only idealized and romanticized but they are also full of contradiction. Portrayed as novel and exciting but also emotionally meaningful and significant, these fictionalized relationships are simultaneously (and impossibly) brand-new and well established! Think Jack and Rose in *Titanic*. We learn that they fell in love and shared an incredibly close bond not long after setting sail, but we are given no explanation for how they arrived at such intimacy. In movie scripts, any undesirable qualities rarely show a negative impact on relationship functioning.[9]

If we make marriage the magic cure to life's problems, we are, in a sense, setting the relationship up for failure.

This unrealistic, contradictory, exaggerated Hollywood love story isn't only targeted at adult audiences. The majority of Disney films portray couples falling in love within a few minutes, getting married, and living happily ever after.[10] Given how impressionable adolescents are (not to mention preschoolers who are watching Disney!), and that approximately 70 to 80 percent of youth look to television and movies for information about love and marriage, this depiction is incredibly problematic.[11] (Keep in mind social learning theory—that we observe others' behavior for insight into how we should behave—and add to it research that finds *we are more likely to imitate behavior if the model is perceived as attractive.* Double whammy.) Are we surprised, then, that research reveals a correlation between romance media consumption and unrealistic, idealistic views of marriage?[12] In other words, the more Disney and romance movies we watch, the more we are setting ourselves up for failure when it comes to intimate relationships and marriage.

Media has so successfully romanticized relationships that we all too easily think of marriage as the end goal. Or the cure-all. The special sauce. We think along these lines:

- *Once I am married, things will be okay.*
- *When I get married, then I will be happy/fulfilled/content/*_____ *(fill in the blank).*
- *These problems will go away once I meet the right person and settle down.*
- *Life will really take off once I get married.*

These underlying assumptions elevate the *idea* of marriage to an unhealthy, unsustainable degree, causing more unnecessary pain and loneliness as a result of singleness *and* marriage. If we make marriage the magic cure to life's problems, we are, in a sense, setting the relationship up for failure and setting ourselves up for disappointment (and potentially divorce). A marriage, and more specifically a person, cannot handle that pressure. And here's the reality: once you get married, you are just that. Married. With the same personality, quirks, frustrations, and goals you had when you were single.

The Effect of Social Media

Social media is another societal shift we must briefly examine, as it too has invaded our culture today and impacts our relational psyche. Social media is redefining intimacy, and electronic devices are replacing face-to-face communication; this electronic invasion can be seen most powerfully in intimate relationships. The line between friendship and romance is more blurred than ever before—are we hooking up, friends with benefits, FBO (Facebook official), or exclusive? Dating, often ruled and regulated by our online lives, has never been so complicated. Relationships begin with carefully crafted facades and depersonalized communication as we put our best online foot forward. Digital stalking prevents us from enjoying the rich unfolding of a nuanced story—flaws and all. It shouldn't be surprising, then, that research reveals a correlation between technology and a false sense of intimacy.

✶ ✶ *When people meet online, they fall for each other two to three times faster than when courtship occurs face-to-face.*

Social media also impacts the ways in which we fall in love. Research indicates that when people meet online, they fall for each other two to three times faster than when courtship occurs face-to-face. Why is this? Because when we don't have nonverbal communication (body language, facial expressions, eye gaze)—which comprises 70 percent of communication—there is much less inhibition. When we foster a relationship over a cell phone or computer screen, it *feels* like an intimate relationship.

Disturbingly, social media also plays a large role in extramarital affairs. Increased opportunities for interpersonal connections, despite physical proximity, has added fuel to the fire of infidelity. Given that opportunity is a key predictor of infidelity, social media has exponentially amplified opportunities for unfaithfulness.

⋆ ⋆ ⋆

"I'm done!" Sarah exclaimed as she bounded into my office. Her face lit up as she spoke about finishing her last final exam the day before. "My family arrives tomorrow; I'm stoked for all of the graduation festivities ahead—even excited about next steps," she said with a knowing smile.

Throughout our time, Sarah and I had worked together to figure out where some of her anxieties and insecurities came from. Having grown up on Disney love stories and unchecked assumptions, she was left to her own whimsical imagination about what life and love would look like as an adult. Couple her romanticism with her country-club upbringing where appearance, status, and success matter, she felt pressure to "do the right thing" and was often worried she wasn't going to measure up. The fact that she was a digital native didn't help either; beautiful pictures and amazing accomplishments of others were only a click away.

"It's so easy for me to get sucked into Instagram, especially late at night; before I realize it, I've spent an hour looking at other's people's picture-perfect posts. If I'm honest with myself, I never feel great afterward. Emotions get the best of me and I feel discouraged and frustrated, like I don't measure up and will never have the life I want." Sarah paused for a moment before adding, "Maybe I'm being dramatic but the whole social media thing is like a deep, dark hole that swallows me."

"Sarah, you're not being dramatic. As we've discussed, you are at a crossroads with many prospects and choices ahead. It's understandable that you feel overwhelmed at times. It makes sense you'd feel 'swallowed' or lost, especially when you begin comparing yourself to others."

Sarah sighed as she referenced an earlier discussion we had and said, "Social comparison really is the thief of joy. I need to remember that and limit myself on social media."

"Yes; you're not alone in that one. Or in any of these challenges. It'll be good for you to remember the work we've done in our sessions together. You've done such a great job of identifying and resetting many of your expectations, realizing that the 'right thing' looks different for each person. You have the tools to navigate what lies ahead and a healthy support system of people who love you. I'm confident you will remain grounded and focused on what matters most to you."

Sarah relaxed into the couch, exhaled, and nodded.

A Biblical Perspective: God's Word to the Rescue

We all want to be grounded and loved for who we are. In a hypersexual, media-infused world that both idolizes and demeans relationships, it's easy for any of us to feel lost and alone. By claiming our true identity as children of God, we anchor ourselves to His good work and steadfast love.

When we fix our eyes on Jesus, we find that love is patient and kind; it does not dishonor, objectify, or sexualize others, nor is it self-seeking. Love does not deceive but rejoices in truth and goodness. Love does not solely exist in marriage, nor is it purely sexual; it is born in friendships and families and involves our whole being. Love does not happen overnight in a bedroom but builds over time as we continue to share our true selves with one another. Love is not purely emotional or rational but is experienced in both body and mind. Love is not transactional, transitory, or conditional; it is a relationship based on mutual attunement, commitment, and care.

★ *Love does not happen overnight in a bedroom but builds over time as we continue to share our true selves with one another.*

Love is an attachment bond, and as I mentioned in chapter 1, I liken it to a dance, full of emotional dialogue and interaction. At our best, we hold each other close, respectful of each other's space but also not afraid to become one. But like even the best professional dancers, we occasionally fall and trip and step on each other's toes. We get hurt. Maybe crushed at times. And then we get up and start over again—at least that is the hope. The dance continues. Partners might change, we learn new steps and moves, and we perfect old ones. We draw close and we step back; we move together in harmony and we go out on our own, proud to do our own thing occasionally. The dance continues, weaving through time and space, yet grounding us in the here and now.

For Christians who put their faith in a triune God, the author of all love, we have assurance that our ultimate dance partner will always protect, always trust, always hope, and always persevere. Christ modeled the greatest act of love through His sacrifice on our behalf, while God the Father shows us mercy and grace, and the Holy Spirit indwells us to infuse our hearts with God's presence and comfort. Given this, may we rest in the assurance that Love has found us and rescued us and accepts us just as we are. May we be grounded in this truth.

Summing Up

- Recent research indicates that our brains are undergoing massive reorganization during adolescence, leading to more coordinated thought and reason. It is not until age twenty-five that our prefrontal cortex, which is home to logic, rationality, and impulse control, is fully developed.

- Discoveries in neuroscience reveal that we rely most heavily on the emotional part of our brain, the amygdala, during adolescence and early adulthood. In other words, emotions win out over logic.

- Couple these brain changes with significant societal shifts—namely the sexualization and objectification of women—and we are at an increased risk for relational and mental health issues. (Objectification is when girls and women are treated as if they were made for others' sexual use rather than seen as people with the capacity for independent action and decision-making.)

- Emerging adults, those ages eighteen to twenty-five, seem to be the most affected by these changes as their brains are reorganizing *and* they are faced with one of the most transitional and exploratory periods of life in which little is normative.

So What?
When we have an increased understanding of the ways in which our brain works and changes, and the unique societal pressures today, we can make better choices—not out of anxiety and fear—regarding love, work, and life.

We are living in a hypersexual world that both idolizes relationships and objectifies young girls and women. Youth and young adults today—whose rational brains are still developing and are therefore more vulnerable to emotions—are bombarded with adult images, unrealistic Hollywood portrayals of love and romance, and social media's depictions of intimacy. Eighteen- to twenty-five-year-olds (emerging adults) are also faced with the most demographic diversity and instability as they navigate a transitional time in life when important changes and choices are made. Combine brain changes, societal shifts, and emerging adulthood, and the immediate result is an incredibly skewed perspective on love, romance, and relationships. Long-term effect? Increased mental health disorders and broken relationships.

If we are aware and mindful, however, of our own vulnerability—both physiologically and psychologically—and the ways in which culture has skewed our perspective on love and romance, we will be more equipped to navigate the many pressures, choices, and decisions during this transitional time of life. And if we choose to fix our eyes above—on the author and perfecter of our faith—we will have the greatest example of how to love well.

Now What? Practical Applications

- Think through your own decision-making style. Are you someone who relies more heavily on logic, or do you tend to go with your gut? Does this vary depending on the type of decision or situation you are in? Be mindful—there is no right or wrong way, and we all utilize both our head and heart; it is beneficial, however, to have insight into your own tendencies so you can better make and evaluate decisions using both thoughts and emotions.
- When you feel overcome by emotions, what do you do to calm down? Is it effective? (If you are in an intimate relationship, ask your partner if it seems effective.)
- Next time your emotions seem to hijack your logical brain, take five long, deep breaths as a way to calm your mind and body.
- Think through some of your favorite movies and social media websites or outlets. How are romantic relationships and love portrayed in them? What about the role of girls and women—how are they depicted? Think along the lines of their appearance, body, and sex appeal. How might these images and ideals impact your own conception of beauty, romance, and relationships?
- What is your perception of love and marriage? What factors helped shape this? What might be some misperceptions you have regarding dating, love, and marriage?
- Think about some of the pressures you currently feel, especially as they relate to relationships. Write at least three down. Where are they coming from? (Recognize that there can be many sources of

pressure, including your own self!) What pressures can you work toward discarding?

- If you are between the ages of eighteen and twenty-five, rest assured that this time in life is both exciting and challenging, full of exploration and change. Give yourself permission to be uncertain and therefore explore, and at the same time, be intentional about working toward your own hopes and goals. And remind yourself that there is no exact, specific timetable or age for marriage!

- What are some differences between Hollywood's depiction of love and Jesus's example? Write down some specific ways in which Jesus loved people around Him. Choose one to focus on this week in your relationships.

Chapter Six

Someday My Prince Will Come

I was thirty-one years old when the man I thought I was going to marry ended our relationship. What began as a college romance spanned eleven years—four on, six off, and one final year of revisiting things "as adults." We cared deeply for each other, so when he called it off, I was crushed, angry, and confused. Although exciting milestones also marked that year—the completion of my postdoctoral fellowship at Harvard Medical School, the passing of the national psychologist licensing exam, and a unique job offer in Santa Barbara, California—I walked down the aisle as a bridesmaid for the *eighth time*, underscoring my fresh and painful single status.

Just after my thirty-second birthday, I packed up my bruised heart, bid farewell to my beloved urban tribe in Boston, and moved to the Golden State, where I had no family and few friends. I wasn't exactly enamored with the palm trees and seeming superficiality of Southern California culture, but the combination of a rescinded job offer in Boston and this exciting job opportunity led me to believe this was the path God was leading me down.

Within a week of my arrival, feeling very much alone already, I developed walking pneumonia *and* begin to receive emails that made it clear others also noticed I was alone:

Dear Andrea,

    I know we haven't officially met, but I enjoyed hearing you introduce yourself at the breakfast gathering the other day. This might seem like an audacious request, but I couldn't help but think you should meet my husband's cousin's best friend. He lives in LA, is about the same age as you, and is a great guy. Would it be okay if I gave him your email address? His name is Rob.

Since I was starting from scratch on all fronts, I waited for my lungs to heal before acquiescing to the setup. First Rob, then Nate, and finally Jason, whose arduous declarations on our second date just about pushed me over the edge. I considered stamping "Single, Not Crazy" on my forehead!

These well-intended but misguided setups through colleagues weren't unique—everyone seemed to express concern over my love life. As though I was broken and needed fixing, my church community back home and family friends would exam my bare left hand for a sparkle that wasn't there. On one hometown visit an older woman said, "Don't worry, sweetie. Someday your prince will come." In response, rather than express my fury, I flashed only the sparkle in my eyes and thought, *I am single, content, and not waiting for a prince, thank you very much!*

Searching for God Knows Who

Ninety-four percent of never-married singles between the ages of twenty and twenty-nine believe that when you marry, it should be to your soul mate. Eighty-eight percent of this same group think there is indeed a special person out there who they would find when they were ready.[1] Young Americans today are on a quest to find that one person who will be just right for them. The prince. The princess. The perfect match. The *one*.

★ *Young Americans today are on a quest to find that one person who will be just right for them.*

Seeking a compatible partner is by no means a twenty-first-century occurrence; humans have paired up since the beginning of time. What is strikingly different today than years past, however, is the soul mate ideal—it has become the most desired marital trait, surpassing religious, social, and economic backgrounds. Responsible? Educated? Of good financial standing? Those things don't seem to matter as much today. Being soul mates takes precedence.

But what exactly does the term mean, and why is the soul mate quest so strong today? Does the soul mate concept have any grounding in marital research and relationship science? Is there biblical support for the soul mate ideal? We'll explore each of these questions in the following sections and find that when we believe we are destined to marry *one* particular person, we are setting ourselves up for more heartache and relational difficulty.

Soul Mate Defined: Two Myths in One

They look deep into each other's eyes and feel an intense, immediate connection. It's them against the world. Their love will conquer all. They have found each other—and it's perfect. He is perfect. She is perfect. They are perfect together, perfect for each other. It's indescribable, just a feeling they both have. It's clear—they have found their soul mate, and they can't imagine life without each other. (Think Nicole Kidman and Ewan McGregor dreamily singing "Come What May" in *Moulin Rouge!*)

Sound familiar? It should. If you are under the age of forty-five and have watched a romantic comedy, tuned in to a pop music station, or enjoyed a typical television sitcom, you've been inundated with cultural messages touting the soul mate credo: there is just one person out there—*designed just for you*—and all you need to do is find each other. So the story goes. Whether it's a Disney classic (*Cinderella, Sleeping Beauty, Beauty and the Beast*) or other blockbuster films (*Sleepless in Seattle, Pretty Woman, Hitch*), the takeaway is the same—when you find your soul mate, you will know you've found "the one."

Not surprisingly, when researchers analyzed two hundred Hollywood romantic comedies, they found a correlation between the problems typically reported by couples in marriage counseling and the very same misconceptions about romance and love depicted on the big screen (such as, "If he loved me, he would automatically know my needs").[2] When we believe there is one perfect person out there just for us, we assume compatibility—as if our partner will automatically know our thoughts, feelings, and desires—and we become frustrated when reality sets in and we have to actually express our needs.

Hollywood isn't alone in propagating the soul mate ideal. Dating apps like Tinder, eharmony, Bumble, OkCupid, and Christian Mingle help you winnow through matches, one swipe at a time, until you find "the one." For over a decade, *The Bachelor* television show has conditioned its national audience to eagerly anticipate the rose ritual—who will be the final recipient? The soul mate claim is proclaimed from all corners.

Upon further examination, this claim comprises two myths:

1. "The one," who I naturally and deeply connect with, is out there.
2. They are the perfect one for me.

We have not just "the one," but "the perfect one." Talk about pressure! This elevates your partner to godlike status and sets him or her, and the relationship, up for failure. We are being sold a distorted version of romance; the problem is that we far too often believe it.

Social media also plays a role in promoting the perfect soul mate claim and distorting our image of reality. Whether it's on Instagram, Facebook, or Twitter, everyone seems to be posting idealized, filtered, and picture-perfect images. From selfies to group shots, vacation snaps or even food pictures, only curated photos are shown and perfection is exalted.

Unlike our grandparents, who lived in a community of many, a growing number of us today live in a community of two.

Today's loneliness epidemic adds to the urgency of finding our soul mate. Twenty-five percent of Americans today say they have no one to confide in about their personal problems, and the number of Americans saying they have only their partner to confide in has risen by 50 percent in the past three decades.[3] We are living in a time of growing emotional isolation. In-person social interaction is declining, the number of social

organizations we belong to is diminishing,[4] and more than ever we live far
from parents, siblings, close friends, and the communities we grew up in.
More people live alone, communicate via a screen, deal with automated
voices or kiosks, and work remotely. Unlike our grandparents, who lived
in a community of many, a growing number of us today live in a community of two. Our partners fill the void by trying to serve as lover, friend,
and community.

It's a dangerous combination—Hollywood's enhanced portrayal of
romance, online dating sites' promise to find us a match, picture-perfect
images posted on social media, and fading face-to-face social connection.
Perhaps, then, we want all the more to believe there is one person out
there who will be our lifeline. This gives us hope.

Toss the List and Notice Your Neighbors!

We all need hope and inspiration. We need stories that help us get through
hard realities. There is a place for the ideal. But when the ideal takes over
reality, we're in trouble. When the majority of Americans believe there
is "the perfect one," the very backbone of our society—loving marriages
and families—begins to fracture. Research indicates that when people
believe they are destined to be with a specific person, they are more likely
to break up, give up, and have difficulty in their relationships. They spend
more time and energy searching for that one specific person than cultivating existing relationships.[5] And when something goes awry—which
inevitably happens in every relationship—they are quicker to call it off
or divorce. They view compromise as settling, become frustrated with
their partner more readily, and are less motivated to make the relationship
work.[6] Research is clear, then—when we believe we are destined for one
soul mate, we're setting ourselves up for disappointment.

*When we believe relationships require effort and
that love grows over time, we have more successful
relationships.*

Instead, when we believe relationships require effort and that love
grows over time, we have more successful relationships. Known as *growth*

beliefs, this line of thinking is in sharp contrast to *destiny beliefs*. People with growth beliefs are more motivated to solve problems, compromise, and explore new ideas in a relationship. When something goes wrong they think, *Better work this out*, as opposed to, *This is not the one—better move on*. Even though people with growth beliefs take longer to commit to a relationship than those with destiny beliefs, their commitment tends to last.[7]

Equally informative as the research on destiny and growth beliefs is what recent studies have found about "the list." Yes, *your* list. Whether you're single, married, or divorced, you've most likely had one at some point. Even if it wasn't actually written, you had an idea in your head about what traits your partner should possess. Your ideal soul mate might be tall, dark, and handsome. Witty, smart, and kind. Wealthy, educated, and from a good family. Adventurous, understanding, and faithful.

*** *Our assumptions about what Mr. or Mrs. Right looks like and the list of traits that "the one" will possess are irrelevant.*

As it turns out, our assumptions about what Mr. or Mrs. Right looks like and the list of traits that "the one" will possess are irrelevant. That's right—throw away the list! When it comes to who will capture our attention at a party or who will be our life partner, the list is totally inconsequential and does nothing for your dating and love life. Research indicates that we are not particularly attracted to those who match our stated ideal characteristics;[8] in real-life encounters, it's factors like rapport and shared humor that are most important.

So what else matters, then? If "the perfect one" doesn't exist, and if we're supposed to get rid of our list, is it just a shot in the dark? There are numerous theories out there regarding how we select our lover. Personally, I like the similarity theory and the propinquity theory. Think "birds of a feather flock together" for the similarity theory, which states that we are more likely to form long-lasting relationships with people who resemble our values; our social, educational, religious, and economic backgrounds; and even our physical attractiveness. Social psychology's propinquity effect states that we tend to form bonds with people we see often; perhaps this explains why so many people end up marrying someone they work with! In other words, shared values and proximity are important when falling in love.

The One: The Rest Are Good Enough

More important than any theory, however, is wisdom gleaned from God's Word. We were created by a relational, triune God to be in fulfilling and significant relationships. God gives us an example of this in His very being—God is one but three distinct persons. Unified yet differentiated. Likewise, we become one with our partner when we get married, yet we remain individually distinct. We call this *differentiation*—the process of maintaining a separate identity while simultaneously being intimately connected in a relationship. We do this not only in our marriages but also in our close friendships and in family life as children develop into their own unique selves. There is unity and uniqueness. Being in close, committed relationships is the primary way, then, that we reflect God's image.

There is nothing in Scripture, though, that suggests we are destined for one specific other. We are forewarned not to marry someone who rejects God (2 Cor. 6:14), and we are admonished to love one another as Christ loved us (John 13:34)—with grace, honor, forgiveness, and commitment—in all of our relationships. Sacrifice and perseverance consistently characterize biblical descriptions of love, as do patience and kindness. Within these parameters and with these admonitions, God gives us lots of freedom to select a partner. Furthermore, Jesus tells us that in this world we will have trouble (John 16:33); perfection doesn't exist this side of heaven. No person is perfect, and no relationship is without flaws. Any partner you choose will hurt you deeply. You will want to hurt them, and you will. Disconnection will happen. It will be hard. For we are all broken and cracked, in need of healing and repair. It is within our most intimate relationships that our cracks are revealed, magnified, *and* healed.

In the mid 1900s, Donald Winnicott, a British pediatrician, introduced the well-known psychological principle of "good enough." Although originally defined in terms of a mother-child relationship, his work has been fundamental to our understanding of mental health. Winnicott stated that the self-accepting state of *good enough* emerges when parents convey to their children affection, acceptance, and appreciation. Mistakes and faults are recognized but are seen as part of the learning process;[9] even though parents might dislike what their children do at times, they are still loved. They are enough. Good enough.

> ✦✦✦ *We are all good enough. As lovers, friends, and family members. Not perfect, but worthy of love regardless.*

We are all good enough. As lovers, friends, and family members. Not perfect, but worthy of love regardless. When we accept this, we work hard and strive for excellence while simultaneously practicing self-kindness. We cultivate relationships and environments that promote growth, not perfection. We are gracious and forgiving, not just to others but also to ourselves.

The takeaway is this: there is no such thing as a perfect soul mate. There is, after all, only one perfect love (1 John 4:7–8, 18). The rest are good enough.

★　★　★

Over a decade ago, when I nursed a broken heart, endured comical setups, and was reassured that "someday my prince would come," I did my best to respond with honesty, grace, and love (not to mention some research data and statistics). I'll have you know that my perfect prince never did come. But my cracked and broken and wonderful husband did. And he is good enough.

Summing Up
- The majority of Americans today believe in the soul mate claim, or destiny beliefs—that there is *one* perfect person they will automatically connect with and are destined to be with.
- Cultural factors—specifically romantic relationships portrayed in movies, music, and television, along with dating apps—promote a

skewed version of romance, contributing to our belief in soul mates. The search for our perfect prince or princess might also arise from a growing fear of being alone, as face-to-face interaction is being replaced by online presence.

• When we believe we are destined to be with one person, we are more likely to give up on relationships; when we believe that people grow together in love, we work harder to maintain the relationship.

• Physical proximity and shared values are two very significant factors in finding one's partner. Research shows that birds of a feather do indeed flock together!

• There is no biblical support for the soul mate claim. Rather our tri-une God Himself is an example of love and relatedness, union and uniqueness. He calls us to love one another sacrificially, with grace, forgiveness, and honor.

So What?

When we have a realistic view of love and romance—specifically about whether there is a soul mate out there for us—we are more likely to have healthy and long-lasting romantic relationships.

Hollywood and online dating sites have duped us. They have led us to believe that there is one perfect person out there, and when we meet him or her, all will be well. Add increasing fears of being physically alone as technology invades our social lives, and we become determined to find our soul mate.

This quest for "the one" doesn't end well. Relationship science reveals that those who believe they are destined for one specific person are more likely to have difficulty in their relationships and to end up getting divorced. When we look for a partner who can grow with us, recognizing that we are all imperfect, we have more long-lasting and committed relationships.

Now What? Practical Applications

• Do you believe there is one specific person out there for you that you are meant to be with? It's okay to answer yes; you wouldn't be alone! Be honest with yourself as you reflect on your beliefs in either destiny or growth.

- If you believe in the soul mate claim, what purpose might it be serving in your own love life? An easy out? Could it be keeping you from committing to or exploring deeper relationships with quality but flawed people? Perhaps it leads to increased disappointment or frustration in your dating life or marriage? Might you be holding your spouse to unrealistic standards?
- What has informed and influenced your belief in either the soul mate claim or the idea that people grow to fit together over time? Are they reliable sources?
- Do you feel like you naturally connect with and understand others, especially your significant other? What thoughts arise in you when you don't feel this way?
- Think about a disagreement you recently had with a partner; how might your thoughts and feelings have been disconnected from one another? How might you have approached the argument differently if you believed understanding is built, not intuitively grasped?
- If someone thought *you* were "the one," what feelings would you experience? Be mindful that although it's natural to feel flattered when adored, no one can uphold the pretense of perfection.

Chapter Seven

You Had Me at Hello

Gordon was confident and assured as he walked into my office. Something was noticeably different in his posture and presentation. I didn't have to wait long to find out.

"I met a girl. And knew right away."

"Knew what?"

"You know, Dr. Gurney, I just knew."

"Knew that . . ." I let my sentence hang in midair. I wanted him to name it.

Gordon was a sharp, conscientious, introverted computer programmer. He hadn't dated much in his twenties, as "it took me a decade to grow up and get my act together." It was clear the desire to be in a relationship was there, but so was trepidation.

"You're going to make me name it, aren't you?" he said as he cracked a smile.

I nodded.

"Fair enough. I am working on being clearer and more assertive in my communication after all. I knew there was chemistry. Something seemed . . . different. I just knew by looking at her; I could feel it in my body. I was attracted to her."

I couldn't help but smile as I playfully said, "So you were experiencing lustful feelings for her right away and that means . . . ?"

Gordon paused and then responded matter-of-factly, as if he was ready for my next question: "I'm not saying it was love at first sight, Dr. G., nor am I thinking marriage yet. Don't worry; I'm still my cautious, calculated, shy self. I'm just saying there was attraction." Then he broke out a sheepish smile and said, "Okay, maybe lust."

"Gordon, there's nothing wrong with physical desire. Let's just name it for what it is and not confuse it with love."

The Science of Love

Over half of Americans believe in the idea of love at first sight. Younger Americans—between the ages of eighteen and twenty-nine—are more susceptible to this belief than those over thirty.[1] Men also seem to be more prone to believe in love at first sight than women.[2] So this naturally leads to the question, Is love at first sight real? One would think so if you've ever listened to music, read a book, or watched Netflix:

- "You had me at hello." (*Jerry Maguire*)
- "The second that I saw you, I knew that we could be great together." (*27 Dresses*)
- "Whoever loved that loved not at first sight?" (Shakespeare, *As You Like It*)
- "The day my life changed forever. . . . The day I first saw you." (Nicholas Sparks, *The Longest Ride*)

We internalize the idea that love is instantaneous and romance, passion, and care will be evident immediately. Words don't necessarily need to be spoken; it could be as simple as a knowing look exchanged or an indescribable gut feeling. Somehow, somewhere, a fleeting gaze registers revelation and foreshadows a bond between two strangers whose fate is suddenly, inextricably linked.

✹ Is love at first sight real?

There is a burgeoning field of research that examines the science of love. Brain imaging allows us to see three distinct areas of our brain that correspond with three types of love, namely lust, romantic love or attraction, and attachment. Before we examine each type of love, note that although there often is a progression from lust to attraction to attachment, not every relationship goes through each stage of love in that particular order.

Skin Deep: Lust

Merriam-Webster Dictionary defines *lust* as "an intense longing" or "a strong feeling of sexual desire."[3] Urban Dictionary nails it: "Often confused with love, it is a purely physical attraction and has no lasting effect."[4] That's right—no lasting effect. Why is this? Because lust, otherwise known as our sex drive, libido, or urge for sexual consummation, can be likened to a mammalian drive, and once satiated, we are done. It's like hunger and thirst. Once the need is met, we move on. Lust is a distinct emotion system regulated by our hypothalamus, associated with primary neural and brain structures.

Pure lust is based on fantasy—the stuff movies are made of. We are surrounded by Hollywood stories of lust that all too often are mistaken for something more. Lust is based on idealization and projection. In other words, we put someone on a pedestal, thinking they can do no wrong and possess every single one of our desired attributes. Beautiful, handsome, sexy, intelligent, funny, hardworking, kind, generous, and the list goes on. Essentially, we think the other is perfect when we are in lust. But here's the problem—we don't actually know the person. Not on a deep level. We just know there's chemistry and attraction.

When we purely lust and remain in this stage of love, we are focused on a person's looks and body. We are more intent on having sex than having conversations. Once the sex is over, we move on with our day. After all, we might not like the real person who could emerge from under the covers. Although we are surrounded by images and ideals of pure lust in our hook-up culture, many of us begin a relationship with a mix of lust and romantic love, desire as well as chemistry and attraction.

Some relationships skip the lust stage altogether—think a deep friendship that years later turns into romance. In that case, there is sense of safety and belonging (attachment) and then one or both partners realize there is attraction. Cue the romance card! Next thing they know, they have desires for one another in a very different way.

Cloud Ten: Feeling High on Love

Next up: romantic love. Anyone who has ever "fallen in love" before knows this one. It's that all-consuming, can't-get-him-or-her-off-my-mind stage. It's also the time when your stomach starts feeling queasy or extra gaseous, your palms get sweaty, and your mouth becomes dry when you're in their presence. (It's a wonder any of us make it past this stage!) You can thank your neurotransmitters, specifically epinephrine (also known as adrenaline), for this bodily reaction. Believe it or not, when you initially "fall" for someone, your stress response gets activated, increasing your blood levels of cortisol and adrenaline.

✦✦ When you initially "fall" for someone, your stress response gets activated, increasing your blood levels of cortisol and adrenaline.

This intense attraction exists in all cultures where data is available. In other words, it is a universal experience. And many of us have been there—for better or worse. Some signs include the following:

- You think about him or her all the time.
- You feel as if you cannot control your passion toward him or her.
- Your lover is special; there is no one else like him or her.
- When adversity strikes, your passionate feelings are intensified.
- Your bodily responses to the loved person are all over the map— from euphoria and exhilaration to anxiety and panic.
- You feel emotionally dependent on the relationship; this includes an inability to concentrate on matters unrelated, fantasies about the beloved, fear of their rejection, and mood swings associated with the fluctuating state of the relationship.
- You desire emotional union with the beloved.
- You focus on the loved one's positive qualities and overlook negative character traits. He or she can do no wrong![5]

From the preceding list, it seems that love can indeed be blinding!

Many of these physiological reactions link to specific neurotransmitters. Along with epinephrine, research examining the brains of newly "lovestruck" couples also indicated a spike in the neurotransmitter dopamine, a chemical associated with desire and pleasure. High levels of dopamine have the same effect on the brain as taking cocaine. That's right—falling in love can be comparable to getting high. Signs of surging dopamine levels in the romantic attraction stage include the need for less sleep, increased energy, intrusive thinking about your lover, focused attention, and feelings of exhilaration.[6] Anthropologist Helen Fisher states:

> Lovers and drug addicts show similar behavior. They both want more. In the case of romantic love, you can't wait to see the person again. You get upset if they don't call you, known as separation anxiety. And when things are going badly, you often lose sleep and don't eat or over eat. People who are in love crave their drug, the beloved; they distort reality, experience personality changes, do dangerous and sometimes inappropriate things and obsessively think about their sweetheart—the center of their world. And when the lover can't win the beloved, or gets dumped, they experience withdrawals and relapse. For drug addicts, drugs are the center of their lives. The same is true for those in love. When it's good, there is nothing better. When it's not good, there is nothing worse.[7]

One last important thing about romantic love—and that is, it activates an emotion category that is distinct from the sex drive. In other words, it goes beyond the fantasy of lust and is focused on a relationship with a specific loved person.

Below the Surface: Love as an Attachment Bond

Finally, let's consider attachment. This is the strong emotional bond between two people who genuinely care for each other. Or, as the Skin Horse in *The Velveteen Rabbit* says:

When a child loves you for a long, long time, not just to play with, but REALLY loves you, then you become Real. . . . It doesn't happen all at once. . . . You become. It takes a long time. That's why it doesn't often happen to people who break easily, or have sharp edges, or who have to be carefully kept. Generally, by the time you are Real, most of your hair has been loved off, and your eyes drop out and you get loose in the joints and very shabby. But these things don't matter at all, because once you are Real, you can't be ugly, except to people who don't understand.[8]

When we are emotionally bonded with each other, love is real. Unlike the Skin Horse, this attachment can—and often does—occur when we have a full head of hair! In other words, we don't need to make it to our fiftieth (or even twentieth) wedding anniversary to be attached. As you may recall from chapter 1, Bowlby's research in the 1950s indicated that attachment first occurs in our early years of life. Since Bowlby's time, psychologists have recognized attachment as a distinct emotion system.

✱✱✱ We are created to thrive in close relationships that stand the test of time.

Oxytocin is the hormone involved in this deep sense of belonging. Oxytocin has been in the spotlight lately and is known as the "love hormone"; it is released during lovemaking, childbirth, and breastfeeding. And get this: humans have a genetic constellation that causes oxytocin receptor sites in the brain to respond to long-term intimacy. In other words, when we are in intimate relationships for the long haul, our oxytocin receptor sites in our brain are activated. Research findings indicate that oxytocin boosts our immune system, lowers blood pressure, and increases wound healing. Clearly, it is life-giving to be attached. We are created to thrive in close relationships that stand the test of time.

Neuroscience research using functional magnetic resonance imaging (fMRI) reveals that we are hardwired for attachment. Let me tell you about one remarkable study that's made a big splash in the field; it's known as the hand-holding experiment.[9] Married women in highly satisfactory marriages were asked to view images of safety and threat while brain images were collected. There were three different conditions: in the first condition, women held the hand of their husband; for the second and third conditions, they either held the hand of an anonymous male experimenter or no hand at all. The results? Women were less stressed when they were holding someone's hand, whether it was a stranger or their spouse. However—and here's the clincher—brain imaging revealed that spousal hand-holding had the most powerful calming influence. The women received significantly more relief and comfort when they were holding the hand of their husbands. In other words, when we are in a healthy love relationship, we are hidden regulators of each other's physiology, emotions, and processing.

Love over a Lifetime: A Game and Brain Changer

So there we have it: three distinct types of love, correlating to specific neural and brain systems. Unlike the many distorted cultural messages portrayed all around us, science reveals that, most often, love grows from passion to intimacy to commitment. True love, in the form of attachment, does not occur instantaneously but rather grows over time. The more we spend time with our partner, the more attractive they become to us.[10] Lust, on the other hand, can occur immediately upon meeting; there is no denying that two people can seemingly "fall" for one another at a moment's glance. If they end up in a relationship, it's simple and easy to say it was love from the start. But let's be clear—it was most likely desire and attraction initially, and their love grew as they actually got to know each other. In other words, lust at first sight can be the basis for a long-lasting love.

Perhaps the most fascinating research that speaks to the ways in which love grows over time are the studies about divorce. Paradoxical, I know, but stick with me! The Institute for American Values conducted a large-scale research project looking at unhappy marriages and divorce, specifically inquiring as to whether divorce makes people happier than staying in an unhappy marriage. Given the high divorce rate in America, it's safe to assume that most of us believe we're better off divorcing than staying in an unhappy marriage. Turns out we're wrong. Findings indicated that unhappily married adults who divorced were no happier than those who stayed unhappily married. (This research did not include relationships where abuse was occurring.) Perhaps more uplifting and inspiring is the fact that two-thirds of unhappy marriages ended up being happy after five years' time.[11]

> ✦✦✦ *Two-thirds of unhappy marriages ended up being happy after five years' time.*

That's right—if we hang in there and stick it out, love will often prevail and we will be happier and more fulfilled as a result. Scientific studies confirm the biblical admonitions to bear with one another in love (Eph. 4:2) and be devoted to one another in love (Rom. 12:10). To "bear with" means to endure, support, carry, or hold up. It means we are to hold each other's hands, for better or worse. We are to stay committed. God's Word stands the test of time.

So what's the takeaway? First impressions matter; pay attention to chemistry. And sparks. Not only are they fun, they might lead to something deeper. *But* chemistry and sexual attraction alone won't suffice. If we believe it does—if we buy into *lust* at first sight—we are limiting our love life. I've worked with young women and men who don't go on a second date because they weren't swept off their feet on the first one. They want to get married, but they don't even go on a second date. That is problematic. Especially since the research is in. And it is as clear as can be: lust often occurs at first sight; true love grows over time.

As a woman of faith, I can't resist drawing parallels between the burgeoning field of relationship science and the age-old wisdom found in the Bible. Research indicates that long-term romance is sustained by attachment, as attachment challenges us to move from self-absorption to attunement with another. It enables us to enter into another's story, truly seeing them with compassion and care. It allows us to connect and stay in the game for the long haul. Likewise, the life and teachings of Jesus tell us to love God with our whole heart, soul, and mind, and to love our neighbor as ourselves (Mark 12:31). More than that, Jesus offers Himself to each one of us (Rev. 3:20); He invites us to be in relationship with Him, reminding us that He will never leave or forsake us (Heb. 13:5). He walks with us, holding our hand each step of the way. Talk about the most trust-worthy, strong, and reliable attachment bond we can have—the constant presence of our everlasting Father.

Summing Up

- The majority of Americans believe in love at first sight—an instanta-neous connection between two people.
- Research indicates there are three distinct stages of love—lust, romantic love or attraction, and attachment—each corresponding with a specific brain region.
- It is possible to have chemistry and sexual attraction with another person immediately, but relationship science indicates that true love is a deep emotional bond that grows over time.

So What?

When we understand that love grows over time as opposed to instantaneously, we are more likely to cultivate and commit to intimate relationships.

We are surrounded by distorted and inaccurate cultural messages about love, one of them being "love at first sight." Although instant physical chemistry and sexual attraction is feasible, it is impossible to love some-one you have only met. Research shows that we become more attracted to a person the more time we spend with them. We should be mindful, then, of confusing lust and love, especially given that we will miss out on opportunities for growth, connection, and true love if we continue to believe in this fairy-tale myth.

Now What? Practical Applications

- Critically examine your own beliefs about love—specifically regard-ing whether romantic love occurs immediately or grows over time. Where do you stand? Why?
- As you listen to the radio, work through your Netflix list, and pick up your next novel, try to identify the types of love portrayed. Are they consistent with your own experience? What about with the research we've reviewed?

- How have your beliefs about love affected your relationships?
- For those who are in the dating world: challenge yourself to go out on a minimum of three dates with a person before making a decision about whether you want to continue seeing them.
- Consider the love stories of couples you admire. How did their romance unfold?
- For those who have put their faith in Christ, meditate on Scripture that affirms His deep love for you, such as Psalm 86:15, Psalm 136:26, Zephaniah 3:17, or John 3:16.

Chapter Eight

Later, at the Castle

"First comes love, then comes marriage, then comes Johnny in the baby carriage" goes the childhood ditty. It makes romantic relationships sound so simple, doesn't it? From kissing (I mean k-i-s-s-i-n-g) we quickly move on to love and marriage. Fairy tales also have famously simplified love. In many of them we see almost formulaic storylines—an initial set of obstacles (mean stepmom, jealous siblings, no dress for the ball) with a quick resolution (pixie dust and fairy godmothers), and *poof*! Off we ride into the sunset, happily ever after.

In today's fairy tales, the struggle always occurs before the romance. Cinderella, orphaned and alone, struggles to survive despite the hatred of her stepmother. Rapunzel, confined in a tower, waits to be released as she strives to discover the truth about her family. Beauty, held captive in an enchanted castle, waits for the evil spell to be broken. Once the spell is broken, justice prevails, true identities are revealed, and the fairy-tale punch line of "happily ever after" brings the story to its end.

These timeless tales are captivating. They are the stories of our youth—perhaps even feeding and nurturing our own romantic fantasies. Unfortunately, too often their unwritten message is that all problems and pain will end in the arms of true love. Once you meet your prince or princess and ride off into the sunset or walk down the aisle, all will be good. Life will be easy, problems will disappear, and your days will be filled with romantic walks, champagne, and rainbows. In other words, happily ever after begins when you marry your true love.

So one version of the story goes.

Reality Hits . . . and Sometimes Hurts

The other version? About 50 percent of us wake up startled, shocked, and surprised. *Where did my prince go? There is someone else sleeping in my bed, eating my food, and calling my children by name. I don't even recognize him. This is not the same person I married. What about my princess? Surely the glass slipper doesn't fit this woman. There's been a mistake. A big mistake. I want out.*

Or maybe another twist in the plot goes like this: *I'm still looking for my prince or princess.* There have been so many balls, so many carriages—all disappointments. Divorce, unwelcome singleness, loneliness, self-doubt, or an overarching feeling of anxiety. The fairy-tale ending has faded into blackness. No hope of a happy ending here. Into the heart of Eden came deception. Temptation. Brokenness. Lies. Then there's Hollywood who, just like the Serpent, has slyly entered the scene, appealed to our relational birthright of loving relationships, and acutely influenced our perceptions. Innocence is gone, reality is skewed, and myths are pervasive. We can no longer be naked and unashamed.

Research indicates that about 50 percent of all marriages end in divorce. The divorce rate for subsequent marriages is even higher.[1] Divorce is the second most stressful life event one can experience.[2] "Growing apart" is one of the top four reasons Americans give for divorcing.[3] For those age forty and older, one of the top reasons given was "simply falling out of love/ no obvious problems."[4] No one moves into the castle with this in mind.

✦✦✦ Marriage almost inevitably evolves from a romance to a working partnership.

When couples beat the odds and remain married, life in the castle still looks different than Eden or Arendelle. The reality is that marriage almost inevitably evolves from a romance to a working partnership. Couples settle into a comfortable routine, and the daily tasks of life come to absorb more time and attention. This shift to the mundane often occurs over the first year of marriage, and research indicates that two years into the marriage, couples focus their activities more on domestic chores and home-based leisure. As the honeymoon fades, couples talk less frequently and for shorter amounts of time, become less openly affectionate—saying "I love you," cuddling, and complimenting each other half as often as when they were newlyweds—and have sexual intercourse half as much.[5] This is the general pattern for most American marriages.

Given this, then, perhaps it's no surprise that in the first year of marriage couples report being highly satisfied, and by the seventh year their satisfaction has dropped significantly. One of the reasons given for this is the notion of habituation—a fancy way to say we get used to each other. The novelty of romance wears off, we settle into a routine, and things become predictable. What used to be romantic—finishing our partner's sentence—has become annoying.

★ *When we expect a happily-ever-after relationship, we are setting ourselves up for disappointment.*

This realistic portrayal of marriage does not, however, need to end in annoyance or broken promises and hearts. At the same time, our love needs to begin with our eyes wide-open, being fully aware that marriage requires work. One of our most beloved cultural myths about marriage is that it is easy. Seventy-eight percent of people believe in elements of the fairy tale when it comes to romance, and research indicates that they experience more angst, devastation, and disillusionment in their relationships than those who gave less credence to fairy tales.[6] The evidence is clear—when we expect a happily-ever-after relationship, we are setting ourselves up for disappointment.

Made for More

Should we slay the fairy tale, then? Ban Cinderella and Prince Charming forever? Look down on those who believe in true love and long for wholeness? No, no, and no! Completely slaying the fairy tale is not what I propose. We want to believe in happily ever after and perfect love; arguably we need to believe in it as it gives us hope in a very broken, fallen world. And ultimately, if we're all honest with ourselves, we long for the fairy tale to come true.

C. S. Lewis wrote, "If I find in myself a desire which no experience in this world can satisfy, the most probable explanation is that I was made for another world."[7] Perhaps, then, our fairy-tale desires are signposts, pointing us to what we cannot yet see (1 Cor. 13:12). Reminding us that there is a Prince who has come from a faraway place to win back His lost treasure. There is a struggle—a fight between good and evil—and an ultimate sacrifice that leads to death. Yes, this Prince is willing to give His very life for His beloved, His chosen people. And He is willing to wait, with a patient and stubborn love, for each one of us to enter into this great love story.

Simultaneously, this Prince has given us one another to love. He never promised it was going to be perfect or easy. As a matter of fact, we were forewarned that the journey would be bumpy (John 16:33; James 1:2–4). There is no storybook ending this side of heaven, and that includes our marriages. Marriage was not designed to be a fairy tale but as a catalyst for mutual sanctification and holiness, bringing each one of us closer to the image of Christ. A reminder, perhaps, that we were indeed made for something more.

The Speck, the Plank, and the Stone

So what does it look like for marriage to be a catalyst for mutual sanctification? How does this fit in with psychological truths and best practices of relationship science?

For anyone who is or has been married, or who has lived with people who are married (think our parents!), we all know one thing—it's possible to despise the one we love. Marriage brings out the best in us and the worst in us. It gives us great joy and causes us deep pain. It comforts us and challenges us, breaks us and builds us. God designed marriage to be a vehicle for change, sharpening each partner to be the person God has intended them to be.

I sometimes think of marriage as an up-close magnifying mirror. When it's going well, the messages are positive and the image is attractive. It feels good to look in the mirror. When it's not going well, what we see is ugly and hard to look at; we want to avert our eyes and run away. And blame our spouse. Yet if we're honest with ourselves, we know it's our own ugliness and sin that is being magnified and staring us in the face. Whether appealing or appalling, the reflected image shows two flawed people, reacting to one another, the outside world, and their own internal dynamics, day in and day out, sometimes over many years.

Marriage forces us to change our natural instincts and habits. The mirror strips away our facades as we discover more about ourselves and our spouse. We see each other's flaws and weaknesses, and if we have the courage and fortitude to stick with it, despite the ugliness at times, we grow and are transformed as a result, becoming more of the person God wants us to be. Tim Keller, in his best-selling book *The Meaning of Marriage*, speaks of marriage as a sanctifying mission.[8] Marriage helps us become more like Jesus—our future glory selves. This is the essence of true friendship and love, helping each other become more holy and Christlike.

It's quite tempting and far easier to focus on the dark side of our spouse rather than our own darkness.

Psychologists think of this transformation as the Michelangelo effect. It's the power that loving, intimate relationships have to sculpt us into the person we want to be. Like Michelangelo's creations, we are asleep within stones, waiting to be discovered.[9] Marriage is one avenue of discovery and confrontation, not only of our spouse but also of our very self.

As masks fall away, it's quite tempting and far easier to focus on the dark side of our spouse rather than our own darkness. And that is precisely what most of us do—we spend time and energy trying to change our spouse, fix their flaws, and point out their mistakes and wrongdoings. This does nothing but harm our marriages[10] and leave a bitter taste in both partners' mouths. For the most part, it's in vain. Sixty-nine percent of couples' problems are perpetual as they are rooted in fundamental personality and lifestyle differences.[11] In other words, these problems are not going away, regardless of the amount of time, effort, and energy we spend arguing over them.

"Why do you look at the speck of sawdust in your brother's eye and pay no attention to the plank in your own eye?" Jesus asked His disciples and the crowd in the Sermon on the Mount (Matt. 7:3). To the Pharisees he warned, "Let any one of you who is without sin be the first to throw a stone" (John 8:7). Thousands of years later, Christ's warning underscores a truth also revealed by research—the most successful marriages are ones in which we actively work on changing ourselves, looking at our own specks and planks, refraining from throwing stones. This could be as simple as softening your tone around heated topics, considering your partner's perspective, or radically extending grace.

Love That Works

We all desire satisfying relationships. It's what we're created for—loving relationships. Yet we need to recognize that love is work and relationships are not static; happily ever after doesn't magically occur. Every single one of us gets disconnected—we lose our balance, step on our partner's toes, and simply miss the mark. Disconnection is, after all, a normal part of the dance. The key questions are: What occurs next? Do we walk away and give up? Do we threaten to leave? Do we harbor resentment toward our partner? Do we resign ourselves and accept detachment as the norm? Do we look for connection elsewhere? Or do we try to repair the relationship, work harder at understanding the other's perspective, and be emotionally present and responsive?

★★★ Love is work and relationships are not static; happily ever after doesn't magically occur.

When we recognize that problems and pain *are* a part of love and that happily ever after doesn't occur automatically, we are more likely to stay committed and invested in our relationships. Conflict and disconnection are a part of true love. Research indicates that the most important factor in predicting a marriage's success or collapse is not the amount of conflict but the amount of emotional expressiveness; when there is a lack of emotional expressiveness and responsiveness, it correlates with the marriage's collapse.[12] One aspect, then, of building happily ever after is the ability to express our needs and respond to our partner's needs. This requires both vulnerability and courage.

Life at the castle looks quite different than what we've been sold. Love that works doesn't require a perfect soul mate with whom we immediately fall in love with and together live happily ever after, but rather it thrives when two broken and fallen people seek to be made holier as they commit to listen well, remain receptive and responsive, forgive often, fight fair, and practice compassion. These are the building blocks that create the formula for a happily ever after.

Summing Up
- Despite our often-believed ideal of living happily ever after, half of all marriages in America end in divorce.
- Marriages require commitment and work, and when we recognize that problems and pain are inherently a part of loving relationships, we are more likely to stay committed.
- Research indicates that when we consistently try to change aspects of our spouse—as opposed to ourselves—we are harming the relationship in the long run.

So What?
When we understand that pain and struggle are a part of true love, and that marriage is a process of mutual sanctification, we are more likely to remain in fulfilling, committed marriages.

A part of each one of us wants to believe in happily ever after. Although this desire points us to something beyond, we need to recognize that on this side of heaven, there is no fairy-tale ending to our romantic relationships. Marriage requires effort and intentionality, and research shows that when we are willing to better ourselves—as opposed to wanting to "fix" the other—we will have happier and longer-lasting relationships.

Now What? Practical Applications
- Do you believe in happily ever after? If so, what does that mean to you and how has it played out in your relationships, or in those around you?

- If you don't fall into the happily-ever-after camp, why not? Have you seen hardship in the relationships or marriages of those around you?
- What are your expectations about relationships? How do they mesh with your partner's expectations? Do you lean toward optimism or pessimism? How about your significant other?
- When you hear that marriage requires work, what is your reaction?
- In what ways are you willing to change and grow in a relationship? What areas of your life would you like sharpened? Share these with your partner.
- Is there something about yourself that you would be unwilling to change, alter, or give up if asked by your partner to do so?
- What have you learned about yourself as a result of your intimate relationships? How have you been shaped and challenged by them?
- Think about people you know who have been married to the same person for most of their adult years. What are some hallmarks of their relationship?

III

PART THREE

Working Toward
Happily Ever After

CHAPTER NINE

Speak the Truth

It was early in the morning and we gathered as a treatment team. The intake information was being read aloud by the chief psychiatrist. "Clients are both in their late twenties, met online six months ago, and are currently struggling with communication problems. Couple currently reside separately but are exploring the possibility of moving in together. They desire counseling to evaluate their compatibility." *Oh, maybe I better not take this one*, I thought to myself; I knew living together before marriage wasn't a neutral topic for me and didn't want my opinions to interfere with the therapeutic work.

My thoughts were interrupted by the chief psychiatrist. "Dr. Gurney, why don't you add Greg and Julie to your caseload," he said with a sly smile. It was as if he had read my mind and wanted to challenge me. I forced a smile in return.

And so my work began. Greg, Julie, and I met weekly for seventy-five-minute sessions. He was a self-employed general contractor. She did marketing for an NGO. They were both from the greater Boston area, born and raised. They were both single and quickly approaching thirty. She wanted to get married; he preferred dating and was "uncertain about commitment." She wanted to move in together, and although he wasn't opposed, his reasons for moving in together were fundamentally different from hers.

115

"I'm happy to shack up, but I don't want her to think it means long-term commitment," he told me in our first session. "I'm not ready for that."

"And I want commitment." Julie was clear about her desire. "If we live together, we'll have a better sense of our compatibility and if this relationship is going to work out."

I refrained from sharing the research about how living together before marriage actually increases one's likelihood of breakup and divorce and instead asked what commitment and compatibility meant to each of them. Come to find out, the root of their problems was not about compatibility; it wasn't about "shacking up" or not—it was about safety.

"I just don't understand what Greg's hang-up is about committing to me. It makes me feel like I'm not good enough to be his wife," Julie said.

"It's not that you aren't wife material—it's just that I'm not ready for that level of commitment. It's not about you—it's about me!" Greg replied.

Neither Greg nor Julie felt emotionally safe in their relationship. Greg expressed a fear that once Julie *really* got to know him, she wouldn't want to be with him. Julie was worried that Greg wasn't being 100 percent honest in his communication with her. In their own ways, each of them felt uncertain and vulnerable. As time passed and they got to know each other better, the stakes felt higher. They felt closer and yet more exposed, and the risk seemed greater. They wanted to be known by the other but were fearful of being rejected.

Safety First

Can't we all relate? Isn't this universal? We yearn to know and be known. Thousands of years ago, the psalmist expressed this desire as well: "You have searched me, Lord, and you know me. . . . You hem me in behind and before, and you lay your hand upon me. Such knowledge is too wonderful for me, too lofty for me to attain" (Ps. 139:1, 5–6). At the core of our being, we want to feel safe and hemmed in—emotionally, physically, and psychologically. We want to belong and, at times, may go to extreme measures to do so.

In 1951, psychologist Solomon Asch conducted what has now become a classic experiment,[1] demonstrating the universal desire to belong and fit in with others. Asch created a "line judgment" task that required participants to evaluate lines of various sizes and assert which lines best matched a particular target line. The correct answer was always very obvious. In each run of the experiment, Asch had a total of about eight participants—but only *one* was an actual subject. The other seven were accomplices—all agreeing in advance what their *wrong* response would be. The single real participant, unaware of this built-in collusion, was required to sit at the end of a line and state his or her answer after all the others spoke. One-third of the participants, even with such obvious correct answers, agreed with the accomplices' incorrect answer. Why? They were fearful of being ridiculed or thought "peculiar." They wanted to belong.

Even sixty years after its inception, I replicate Asch's line judgment task with the students in my general psychology classes. Sure enough, a surprising number of today's college students still give a wrong answer rather than deviate from the group. They are fearful of being laughed at by their classmates.

When we give up our true voice to please another or conform to the group, we miss opportunities for genuine exchange and intimacy.

We want to fit in. Moreover, we fear rejection. So we conform, we remain quiet, we don't always communicate honestly. Or we don't communicate at all. But this comes at a cost: when we give up our true voice to please another or conform to the group, we miss opportunities for genuine exchange and intimacy.

Known and Loved

Over the past two decades of working with couples and families, I have found two overarching reasons that we do not communicate directly and honestly with one another: rejection and retaliation. We are afraid of losing another's love, and we are fearful of retribution.

"To be known and not loved is our greatest fear."[2] This fear is so great, we would rather be loved and not known. Said another way, our desire to be welcomed, included, adored, and needed is so overwhelming that in the face of conflict we choose the path of least resistance and avoid speaking the truth. Silence, or a watered-down version of the truth, becomes our default mode of communication. We fear that honest expression of our feelings—especially "negative" feelings such as anger and hurt—might cause the other to be angry and withdraw. For some, that is too much to bear.

Others have learned to "stuff" their negative feelings—silencing them even in their own head. Communication that is not positive, after all, must not be productive. Or so we are taught. Often this misconception is learned at a young age when families shelter children from "negative" emotions. "If you don't have anything nice to say, don't say anything at all" is a common parenting refrain. Children come to believe that frustration and anger are not "good" and shouldn't be spoken about, let alone directed toward another. We learn to keep certain emotions to ourselves, confined and locked tightly within our heart and head. There will be a cost if we are honest, and the punishment of rejection outweighs any benefit— or so we are led to believe.

Some adults develop an inflated view of their anger's strength. From an early age, they've imbued emotions with the power to hurt or destroy. "It's my fault my parents divorced. I shouldn't have argued about my bedtime." These internalized feelings, which can cause children to assume blame and potential guilt, often cause emotional withdrawal from their family. Fast-forward twenty years and we've got young adults who feel panicked by the thought of being honest with their feelings; this can be the root of adult anxiety and depression.

*✶ *We worry that if we speak truthfully about difficult personal topics, there will be a counterattack.*

Alongside rejection, the second main reason for less-than-honest communication is fear of retaliation—an "I'll get you back" attitude. Spoken or unspoken, this fear can be powerful. Whether in friendships, work relationships, parent-child dyads, or marriages, we worry that if we speak truthfully about difficult personal topics, there will be a counterattack. Revenge, however subtle or blatant, is a reality. What do many of us do, after all, when we are the recipients of these difficult messages? We get defensive and we shift the focus to the other; we defend, deflect, and derail. We make it about the other's shortcomings or faults. In essence, we retaliate, often without knowing that's what we are doing.

How different would it be if we could put aside our own fears, let alone experiences of rejection and retaliation, and be honest with one another? For many, this requires revisiting the lessons learned in our family life. What were the emotional exchanges that occurred in your family of origin? Was crying allowed? How about anger, frustration, and envy? How did your parents respond to your emotions? Were negative feelings welcomed and talked about, or were they immediately shut down and forbidden—viewed as wrong, bad, or sinful? Were mixed messages prevalent? For example, was "Of course I love you" yelled in an angry tone? Did words match feelings?

"I remember my mom wincing when I got angry," Greg shared in one of our sessions. "Or she would cry and fall apart. She just couldn't handle it." He learned that anger was indeed powerful and could destroy. "We weren't allowed to disagree with my parents, especially my father. It was his way or the highway; we didn't question his authority out of fear of getting punished or shamed." Greg learned that anger was unacceptable, and disagreeing was toxic to oneself and relationships.

Strong feelings do not disappear, even when they are ignored or prohibited. They simply get repressed, and often become stronger and take on a life of their own, with or without the person knowing it. This creates confusion and fear. But when we name and acknowledge our emotions— and when someone responds with empathy to them—they become less intense.

We need to learn, ideally as children, that feelings will not overpower or be toxic to a relationship. Feelings will not destroy. However intense, powerful, or negative one might feel, the other person can handle it. If they can't, we need to calmly remind ourselves that our broken world often falls short, and we are not responsible for others' emotions or coping skills, or whether they continue to choose us through difficult times. When we see that people are bigger than feelings and that negative emotions can be safely handled, we are able to enter into genuine relationships without fear of rejection or retaliation. When we give ourselves permission to be angry, we are being sincere, and we can be open and nondefensive when responding. This knowledge and freedom promotes confidence in ourselves and in our relationships.

Safety First, Second, and Third

But how, specifically, can we communicate in a safe and honest way? Let me outline four specific principles that promote healthy, intimate, and truthful dialogue.

Principle One: Accept

The first step might be the hardest: acceptance. We need to fully accept all feelings, even the ones that are hard for us to hear because they relate to our shortcomings. We need to allow others (and ourselves!) the freedom to feel angry, frustrated, cheated, or used. This is most challenging when anger or frustration is directed at us personally. "I didn't mean to make you feel angry" or "I didn't say that" is often our immediate response. But what's the problem here? Not only have we made it about ourselves as we try to defend our position, we have failed to accept the other person's feeling of anger. We have dismissed their emotion and are focusing on our intentions. Our attempt to apologize, then, leads to more anger and sadness.

Regardless of the cause of the hurt or anger, the message needs to remain the same—*all* feelings are acceptable. Our children, parents, friends, lovers, spouses, and siblings are allowed to feel whatever they want. It *is* okay to be angry at someone, to even feel contempt toward them. Even Jesus got angry. However, it is not okay to tell someone they are incompetent or to behave aggressively toward them. In other words, all feelings are acceptable, but the expression of feelings has certain limits.

✦ *All feelings are acceptable.*

One of my clients, an insightful twenty-four-year-old psychology graduate student, related this story to me the other day. "I was driving home enraged. My mother had just hung up on me after accusing me of inappropriately meddling in my sister's life. I wanted to call her back and scream, yell, and curse at her. Then that all-powerful message from my childhood and adolescent years echoed loudly in my head: 'You must respect me; I am your parent.' I was the 'bad one' here for being mad at my mom. As if someone was audibly yelling that I was bad, I yelled back with urgency and volume, 'Stop!' I had to pull over and take a couple of deep breaths. Then, on the side of the road, I thought of you. 'What would Dr. Gurney say?'" She softened and smiled. "I answered my own question as I said out loud, 'Dr. Gurney would say it is okay to be feeling this way . . . I can feel angry and infuriated with Mom. It is allowed. Yes, I am certain she would want me to accept my anger.'"

I nodded. She was spot on. Not only did I want her to accept and embrace her own strong feelings of infuriation, I wanted her to know it was a reasonable and healthy reaction.

Whether it's your own feelings of anger, or anger directed at you, acceptance is key. Depending on your temperament, family history, and culture, it can be challenging to actually put acceptance into practice. The stronger the hurt, pain, or anger, the harder it is to fully embrace it. The best way to accept the other's feelings is by simply naming it. "You are angry," "You feel hurt," and "It seems like you are feeling shamed by me" are examples.

Principle Two: Empathize

After accepting the feeling, we need to try to identify with it. Empathy is the capacity to recognize emotions that are being experienced by another person; it's the attempt to put ourselves in the other's shoes, to look beyond our view and see their perspective. As we work to make communication safe, we must keep in mind that all perspectives, however foreign they might seem in the moment, are valid.

Even if we cannot understand the other's emotional reaction, or we feel they are overreacting, we can, at the very least, *recognize* the emotion. We all know what it's like to feel enraged, shamed, jealous, fearful, frustrated, or hopeless. Experiencing these emotions is familiar territory for all of us; recognizing them in our partner is the challenge and the opportunity for deep empathy and greater intimacy. As a couples therapist, I see this challenge play out all the time.

"Every time I come home and share about my stressful day, Todd has to problem solve. All I want to do is vent—and all he wants to do is fix it," exclaimed Anna.

"But how can you blame me? I'm only trying to help! It's always the same thing. Your workload is too much and your boss is a jerk. You need to stand up to him and set boundaries," Todd quickly replied.

"I spent two years in grad school and have only been on the job for six months—what are my options? Just saying no to my boss or leaving work undone isn't the answer," responded Anna.

Anna started down the path that Todd led her on, one that bypassed her feelings and became solution-focused. This pattern is almost universal because we so quickly want to help the person we love. In jumping to problem-solving, though, we fail to see the heart of the issue, thus missing out on an opportunity for deeper understanding of the other.

I could see that Anna felt shut down and Todd felt misunderstood, so I modeled empathetic listening and said, "Anna, that's so hard. It sounds like you feel stuck in a job that's such a grind. You must feel frustrated—like your hands are tied. Maybe even a little helpless?"

Anna quietly nodded and her expression softened. Todd noticed her body relax, reached over and grabbed her hand, and said, "I'm sorry, babe. That sucks." The whole tone of the room changed as she felt validated and understood.

We all want to be understood. So step two in making communication safe is to empathize—put yourself in the other person's shoes and connect with their emotion. If you are the recipient of their anger or frustration, empathy and connection is often more challenging. Sentences that begin with "It sounds like you are feeling . . ." or "I hear you saying that . . ." are good launching points, but they should be followed by your *emotional* response (e.g., "That must be so hard," "That makes me so sad that you feel that way," "I am so sorry to hear that"). You must make an attempt to understand and verbalize their perspective, and, most importantly, relate to it. Join with their emotion. If you miss the mark on their specific emotional state, they will let you know, and you can try again to understand and validate. Rather than making assumptions, take on a posture of curiosity to help them articulate—and help you understand—what they are feeling. Ask questions until you both understand what is really on the table. Once you have understood and empathized, then you can explain your position by sharing your perspective or help them solve the problem if they are open to feedback.

Why is empathizing so important? It makes a connection and lets the other know they are heard. When we feel heard, we are more centered and grounded. Our emotional brain settles down when we feel understood. Research with fMRIs indicates this to be literally true; our amygdala—which spikes when we are emotionally flooded—flatlines when someone validates our perspective! Our loneliness dissipates. Our mind opens up to possibilities. We are able to listen, receive advice, and solve problems once we feel heard and understood.

Principle Three: Contain
"I get it. I get it. I hear you." Greg's voice was firm yet nurturing as he reached over to give Julie a hug. He held her for at least a minute or two as the room fell silent.

Beautiful, I thought. This is just what Julie needed, especially from him. The tension that filled the air subsided, and a sense of safety now permeated the space between this couple. He was able to contain her—both physically and emotionally. I was thrilled. Progress!

We all need to be contained. For most of us, we have learned how to contain ourselves, how to bear the experience of being ourselves. We recognize signs of stress and overload, and we employ effective coping skills. When we are feeling emotionally distraught, we know how to talk ourselves down and restore emotional equilibrium. In intimate relationships, we come to learn how to contain the other; often, understanding and affirmation are key.

✦✦ *Managing overwhelming emotions is not innate.*

But managing overwhelming emotions is not innate. We learn how to do this as children—or at least that is the hope. Intense and unmanageable feelings occur frequently in childhood; it's part of our central nervous system developing. In order for us as children to begin to manage our primitive, inarticulate feelings, we need repeated, reliable experiences of an understanding, empathetic listener. In other words, we need to be comforted. When a caregiver responds to our distress by listening, holding us, and simply being a supportive presence, this enables us to feel held and contained as overwhelming feelings become manageable. This parental containment is then internalized and provides a secure base from which we begin to contain ourselves.

If we grow up in emotionally restricted environments, however, emotional growth is stunted. Neural networks and pathways are underdeveloped and brain regions show abnormalities; neuroimaging studies of children who grow up in chaotic or neglected environments confirm that brain development is use-dependent, meaning that it changes in response to repetitive activation.[3] Given that the brain is a historical organ and reflects our personal story and history, we then grow into adults with an underdeveloped capacity to make sense of emotional experiences. Communication—especially regarding emotions—is not inherently safe. Add negativity to the mix, and we feel flooded—overwhelmed and shellshocked. Our heart rate and blood pressure peak, and adrenaline secretions trigger the fight-or-flight reaction.

For many of us, then, learning to trust—not only ourselves but also the other—with our emotional experiences is a process. We need patterned, repetitive experiences in safe and predictable environments to activate certain brain regions that are otherwise dormant. In other words, we need caring, supportive, and nurturing relationships. Regardless of our background, we all need supportive and trusting relationships in which we can bear the experience of being ourselves, comfortably move through intense emotions, and help contain one another when emotions run high.

Principle Four: Structure
After we have accepted, empathized with, and contained the other, we now need to provide some structure. We need boundaries to help us navigate intimate conversations, especially when emotions are intense. For the most part, these are the basics of being polite in a conversation—no interrupting, use *I* statements (we'll discuss the specifics of *I* statements in chapter 10), wait your turn, be respectful, and tell the truth. These

lessons seem a lot harder to live out in our intimate adult relationships. We tend to be extreme in our communication when our amygdala has taken over—we either attack and defend or sugarcoat and back down. And we interrupt often. "You're the one who's always making us late!" "You said this to me; how was I supposed to respond?" We must have structure and rules in communication, as this fosters honest and intimate exchanges and, when we disagree, helps us fight fair (which we will explicitly talk about in the next chapter).

⁑* *We need boundaries to help us navigate intimate conversations, especially when emotions are intense.*

Just yesterday I made a new rule with a couple I've been working with for five months. We had already established the speaker-listener technique[4]—one person starts off as the speaker (using *I* statements), and the other's role is to attentively listen and, when the time comes, paraphrase what they heard their partner saying, ask if their interpretation is correct, and if so, the roles switch. (The thinking behind the speaker-listener technique is twofold. One, we must slow down communication, especially when emotions and thoughts are flying high. And two, understanding must precede a response; when we truly hear what our partner is saying and the emotion behind it, our response often looks quite different than what it would have been.) But in the most recent session I learned that the wife's "new tactic during our arguments" was to threaten divorce. So a new rule needed to be added: "The *D* word is off-limits as long as we are working together."

When we think of providing structure as the last step in making communication safe, let us be mindful of our approach. We must come to the table with clear rules and boundaries. Limits and love are not mutually exclusive; they go hand in hand. We must be honest. Pastor and author Tim Keller writes, "Love without truth is sentimentality; it supports and affirms us but keeps us in denial about our flaws. Truth without love is harshness; it gives us information but in such a way that we cannot really hear it."[5] Honest communication requires speaking the truth in love.

* * *

My work with Greg and Julie continued. We worked backward, in a way, and started with the ending. What did each desire in their relationship? What were their hopes and expectations? Like many of us, they were hesitant to name expectations; it's as if they were trying to protect themselves from disappointment resulting from unmet hopes. Greg appeared easygoing and casual about his hopes, as if they didn't really matter, and Julie stated what she desired (commitment) but shied away from naming her true hope—commitment to and from Greg. It wasn't just anyone she wanted to commit to; she wanted to be with Greg.

Session after session, they became increasingly honest and vulnerable with each other. Emotions became less overpowering or useless as Greg and Julie became more skilled at expressing and accepting them. As they became more real and raw in the presence of the other, connection and empathy followed. Containing the other didn't come as easily, though; they had a hard time bearing the other's pain. It was unfamiliar territory for Greg, and for Julie it triggered a more frightening place, a part of her story that was hard to revisit. Active listening, validation, and empathy were crucial; remaining in the moment, open to each other despite the unvarnished truth, was their lifeline and course of healing. Despite their woundedness, or perhaps because of it, they became wounded healers. It was a beautiful thing to bear witness to.

Regardless of my wounds, failures, and mistakes, God loves me.

As a person of faith, I have tremendous peace and confidence in God's unchanging love for me. Regardless of my wounds, failures, and mistakes, God loves me. However stubborn, judgmental, and prideful I am, God loves me. Despite my messy, complicated self, God loves me. God loves *me* with an everlasting, never-changing love. He knows my heart, and still He loves me. I am known *and* loved by the Creator of the universe. He won't leave me. "For I am the LORD your God who takes hold of your right hand and says to you, Do not fear; I will help you" (Isa. 41:13). I rest in this incredible promise. May we all be able to rest and find freedom in the knowledge that someone bigger than us loves us and has our back. When we are known and loved unconditionally, rejection becomes an impossibility, and we gain confidence and freedom to express ourselves without fear.

Summing Up

- We all want to be known and loved. At times, we're willing to give up some of our own voice in order to belong; this comes at a cost.
- Underpinning a majority of relational challenges and poor communication is the fear of rejection or retaliation.
- When emotions and thoughts are intense or considered "negative," we often forget some of the basic principles of communication and resort to unhealthy strategies such as defending ourselves, attacking the other, ignoring, or sugarcoating.
- When we accept that all feelings are valid, empathize and connect with the emotion, provide an emotionally safe space, and structure the conversation in order to work through our thoughts and feelings, we promote honest communication. This fosters security and intimacy in a relationship.

So What?

When we take the time to communicate honestly and openly, seeking not just to be understood but to understand, we grow closer to one another, navigate relational problems more successfully, and feel safe, known, and loved.

Authentic and forthright communication is one of the cornerstones for healthy relationships. More often than not, though, when anger, hurt, disappointment, or disagreement occur in our intimate relationships, we rely on ineffective communication strategies such as blaming, defending, or sugarcoating. We must learn and practice how to engage in intentional, honest communication for our relationships to grow in love.

Now What? Practical Applications

- When intense feelings of hurt, anger, or disappointment arise in your relationships, what do you do? How do you handle your own intense emotions? What about the other person's emotions? Is there a pattern or tendency you have noticed in the way you react? Do you avoid? Defend? Blame? Brush it off? Make it nice?

- What were the spoken and unspoken messages about intense, "hard" feelings in your family of origin? How might that be affecting your communication today?
- Practice naming your truth in love. Over and over. If you are worried about how the other person might take it, name that. For example, "I'm nervous that you are going to get upset by what I have to say, and that is not my intent. I simply want to share my perspective, and I'm working on expressing my true feelings." You can even add, "This is more about me and where I'm coming from than you."
- Actively listen. When you next find yourself in an intense conversation, put aside your own agenda or your worry about what you might say, and simply listen. Attentively. Then listen some more. Remember that everyone needs to be heard and affirmed, without judgment or interruption.
- Practice the speaker-listener technique. Remember the basic rules:
  - » Only one person at a time is the speaker; the other is the listener. It can be helpful for the speaker to hold something (such as a pen) as a visible reminder of who the speaker is.
  - » The speaker is to use *I* statements and speak only for themselves, not trying to anticipate what the listener is thinking. After the speaker has spoken for a bit, pause and let the listener paraphrase what was just said.
  - » After the listener paraphrases, the listener should confirm understanding by saying something such as, "Is that right?" or, "Did I get all of it?" If the speaker responds affirmatively, then the listener now becomes the speaker; the pen is passed and the process is repeated.
  - » If the speaker feels the listener's paraphrase wasn't quite right, the speaker needs to try explaining again, perhaps using different words. The listener needs to paraphrase what he or she heard and ask whether the information was understood accurately that time. Once there is clarity, the roles can be switched.

- Be intentional about acknowledging and validating the other person's perspective. Recognize their point of view as valid to them, even if you don't agree with it.
- Think through three specific steps you can take to improve communication in your relationships. Write them down and share them with another. And then get busy putting them into practice!

CHAPTER TEN

Fight Fair and Forgive Often

It was our third of six premarital counseling sessions when Madison proudly and energetically said, "We haven't had one fight or disagreement yet, actually." Mark nodded in agreement; I raised both my eyebrows in surprise. What they saw as a healthy, positive sign, I viewed as a potential red flag. If there were no disagreements, there were no opportunities to learn about one of the essentials of marriage—and that is how to fight fair.

Conflict without resolution leads to a harmonious relationship; conflict with resolution results in intimacy.

Conflict is inevitable in a long-standing intimate relationship—whether that be with a partner, parent, friend, or sibling. It is going to happen; it's just a matter of how frequently. And, more importantly, how well we handle it, *if* we handle it at all. In my clinical work over the past two decades, I have discovered that some individuals, couples, and families choose harmony over intimacy. Don't get me wrong—harmony *sounds* oh-so-wonderful. But note the distinction between harmony and intimacy when it comes to conflict in our relationships. In harmonious relationships, people get along well and rarely fight. When conflict is brewing, they either avoid it or sweep it under the rug and ignore it. And then move on. They keep the peace at all costs because harmony is a safe choice.

In intimate relationships, grievances and disagreements are aired, not avoided, as we seek to understand, empathize, and have compassion. When conflict is afoot, those who choose intimacy face it. Some even welcome it, knowing they feel closer to the other after it's worked through. The main difference between harmony and intimacy, then, is how we handle conflict—conflict without resolution leads to a harmonious relationship; conflict with resolution results in intimacy.

Pick Your Poison: Fight, Flight, or Freeze

Think about your last fight. What happened? How did you respond? Which of the following did you do?

1. Walked away in the middle of it.
2. Avoided and denied it altogether by simply saying something along the lines of, "I don't want to have this conversation; let's just forget about it; everything will be okay and work itself out."
3. Gave in quickly and said, "I'm sorry, I guess you are right," even though you didn't really believe that.
4. Fought back, whether by criticizing, blaming, dominating, becoming defensive, complaining, name-calling, or using sarcasm or some other aggressive act.
5. Appeared calm and quiet, although you were angry on the inside (i.e., resorted to the silent treatment).

These are all "normal" emotional reactions to feelings of threat or stress. And when conflict occurs in our intimate relationships, our fear response is triggered. Whether we fear getting hurt, being wrong, losing, experiencing rejection, or being controlled, our stress response is activated and stress hormones flood our body, prepping us for what's to come. Blood leaves our brain (leaving us less rational) and heads into our arms and legs, once again getting us ready for action—to fight, flee, or freeze. This is incredibly helpful if a bear or a bag snatcher is coming at us; it's not so great, though, when we're in conflict with our partner or family member. Our instinctive, emotional brain (remember the good ole amygdala) takes over while our rational, problem-solving cerebrum shuts down.

The first physiological response is to fight back. Adrenaline primes us to duke it out, so we defend, blame, bully, intimidate, insult, compete, or verbally attack our partner. This is a defensive, self-protective response in which we are moving against the other. If, on the other hand, we quickly surmise that we can't win the fight—our partner is too powerful—then we flee. We never even engage in the conflict. We avoid it by withdrawing, ignoring, postponing, denying, or shifting blame. (An example of shifting blame would be, "If you didn't make me so angry, I wouldn't have to leave.") In essence, we run. If, however, we feel like we can't win or outrun, we freeze. This is the third, seemingly automatic, physiological stress and fear response. We feel panicked and helpless, and as a result we become numb and immobilized. We become disengaged. We're like a deer in the headlights, frozen and wishing we could disappear. The freeze response tends to happen when we're terrified and feel hopeless, as if there's no chance for escape.

Here Come the Horsemen

If our fight-flight-freeze response wasn't enough to contend with, we've also got to be mindful of the "four horsemen." Leading couples therapist and researcher John Gottman is known for using the phrase "Four Horsemen of the Apocalypse" to describe four interpersonal styles that lead to marital discord—criticism, contempt, defensiveness, and stonewalling.[1] He, like many others, believes that the way a couple deals with conflict can be indicative of whether the relationship will last. Just like we have to be knowledgeable and aware of our stress response, we must be mindful of any "horsemen-esque" tendencies. It's important to note: we don't need to be dating or married to use one of these horsemen! Let's briefly look at each one.

Criticism
The first and most commonly used horseman is criticism. A criticism is a global statement with which we essentially attack and blame the other.

Generalized statements such as "You always . . ." or "You're the type of person who . . ." are examples of the way critical statements begin. They go after your partner's character and escalate and globalize the problem. It is important to distinguish *criticizing* from *critiquing* or even *complaining*; the latter two are about specific matters and are fair game when fighting. Notice the difference:

> *Complaint*: "I'm aggravated you didn't call to let me know you were going to be late; I could have rearranged things had I known."
>
> *Criticism*: "You can't be counted on to be on time! You're selfish and inconsiderate—never thinking about how your actions affect others."

Contempt

Having contempt ups the ante on criticism, as it is an attack on the other's sense of self with the intention of insulting him or her. This can involve name-calling, sneering, mockery, hostile humor, and body language such as eye rolling. It's when we are plain old mean. And condescending. It communicates disgust and is disrespectful.

> *You're burned out? Give me a break. I, too, have a demanding full-time job* and *I'm the one doing all of the housework, while all you do after work is sit around and watch stupid shows, expecting that the laundry and dinner will get done automatically. You're pathetic.*

Contempt is ignited by long-standing negative thoughts about your partner and is more predictive of divorce than criticism.[2] Additionally, couples who are contemptuous—who have deep and long-lasting anger— have weakened immune systems and are more likely to get sick and catch common colds.[3]

Defensiveness

We're all familiar with the third horseman—defensiveness. This is a frequent go-to response when we feel unjustly (and sometimes justly!)

accused. We avoid taking responsibility, fish for excuses, disagree, cross-complain (meeting your partner's complaint with a complaint of your own), or "yes-but." We say things like this:

- *Don't get upset with me about being late. You're the one who is always running behind schedule.*
- *What are you talking about? I don't sit around and watch TV all the time. You're totally off base.*

In effect, defensiveness is when we blow off the other and attempt to ward off a perceived attack by placing blame on them instead.

Stonewalling

Lastly there is stonewalling—mentally checking out of the relationship. More often than not, men employ this horseman; they withdraw and disengage from the relationship as a way to avoid conflict. They are non-responsive and silent. Partners, family members, and friends may think they are trying to be "neutral," but stonewalling conveys disapproval, icy distance, separation, and disconnection. By avoiding the conflict, one is, in essence, avoiding the relationship.

Ten Tools for Fighting Fair

We need to be aware of our own fight-flight-freeze tendency as well as the four horsemen in order to practice effective communication when conflict arises in any of our relationships. Respecting and nurturing our relationships involve fighting fairly and fighting well. Here are some over-arching principles that can help you as you navigate your next heated conversation.

Make I Statements

Simple but true, we all need to remember to use *I* statements. Effective *I* statements have three components: your feelings; a brief, nonblame-ful description of the behavior you are annoyed at; and the effect of the behavior on you. For example, "I'm annoyed that you didn't get home on time because that means all the responsibility for the kids falls on my shoulders." You can even add what I call a "next time" statement, such as, "Next time can you call and let me know you're going to be late?" Remembering to use specific *I* statements is a helpful antidote to criticism because we are expressing our feelings without pointing fingers at the other, and the conversation begins in a gentler, nonaccusatory way.

Claim Responsibility

Another basic-but-oh-so-hard-to-live-out principle: own your part. Or as my kindergartener says, "When you mess up, fess up!" That's right—claim responsibility for your words and actions. When you are next in a conflict, ask yourself, "What is my role in this?" "What can I do about it?" and "What can I learn?" When we claim responsibility, it is hard to be defensive and easier to be forgiven.

Be Aware of Your Attributions

Social psychology research indicates that when we are explaining another's behavior, we tend to overestimate their personality traits and underestimate the importance of the situation. (This is known as the fundamental attribution error.) When we're frustrated with our partner, we often attribute their "bad behavior" to their personhood and fail to take into account the situation. "You're just someone who runs late; you don't have a good sense of time management or planning." Interestingly enough, however, when explaining our own shortcomings, we look to external factors; in other words, we blame the situation. "I was late because I was stuck behind the slowest car ever." Clever of us, eh? Just think how automatically and quickly we shift the blame depending on who is committing the infraction. Often, without conscious awareness, we are judging our partner as inherently flawed.

When we're frustrated with our partner, we often attribute their "bad behavior" to their personhood and fail to take into account the situation.

In the face of conflict and disagreement, we must ask ourselves, Am I viewing my partner's behavior in the most positive way? Am I giving them the benefit of the doubt? Am I extending them the same grace I extend myself? It behooves us to be slow to judge, quick to listen, and open to considering situational factors when conflict occurs.

Build Appreciation

Ever notice that when you are talking to your partner or a family member (as opposed to an acquaintance or work colleague), it's easier to be unkind and sometimes even disrespectful? Why is it that those we love the most are those we are potentially the harshest and most unpleasant to? Feeling safe in a relationship does not give us the license to be rude and hostile. All relationships are liable to damage and therefore require nurturing and care, especially during times of conflict.

> *We need to remind ourselves that the person in front of us, who is potentially driving us crazy, is worthy of honor and respect.*

We need to remind ourselves that the person in front of us, who is potentially driving us crazy, is worthy of honor and respect. By maintaining a sense of respect for the other, we are less likely to be contemptuous toward them in conflict. It's helpful to remember—and communicate—the positive qualities that we love, appreciate, and are grateful for in our partners. Practice sharing admirations, compliments, and appreciations on a daily basis with your partner. Like making deposits in the bank, you are storing up positive thoughts and feelings about the other that will serve as a buffer and guide, helping you navigate more thoughtfully and affectionately during times of conflict.

Take a Time-Out

This is a simple one—take a break when needed! When you feel yourself getting emotionally or physiologically overwhelmed, stop the conflict discussion and let your partner know you need a break. Take at least twenty minutes, as this is how long it takes for our body to physiologically calm down after our stress hormones are triggered.[4] And breathe. Rhythmically and smoothly inhale to a count of four and exhale to a count of four. No perseverating on the conflict, no thinking about what you can say next, no righteous indignation, and no obsessing over what went wrong. Simple breathing. This helps reestablish equilibrium and restore our ability to think, listen, and relate. Every once in a while, we *all* need a time-out.

Accept Influence and Be Teachable

We are all malleable—works in progress. Shaped and molded by our life experiences—but most refined by our intimate relationships. Marriage brings two people into closer contact than any other relationship; the parent-child relationship is a close second, but there is a major power differential there. It is within marriage that the truth of each individual comes out—the good and the hard, our strengths and our flaws, the dross and the gold. We all need refining, and both husbands and wives need to be open to the other's sharpening. Research shows women are more likely to let their husbands influence them by taking their opinions and feelings into account; it's much more difficult for husbands to share power and be influenced by their wives.[5] Yet, when both men and women are open to accepting influence and being persuaded by the other, the result is stronger, happier marriages.[6] After all, accepting influence is acknowledging that the other's viewpoint is valid and that their needs are important; this is key to remember during times of conflict when we need to be influenced, sharpened, and teachable.

Keep Short Accounts

Air your grievances (at least the significant ones) when they occur; don't stockpile. When we stockpile hurts, resentment builds. I find far too many people don't let their partners know the ways they've felt hurt, betrayed, embarrassed, or shamed by them. Instead, they try to brush it off, get over it on their own, or simply forget about it. The problem is that relational problems and frustrations aren't solved individually; we hurt *and* heal in relationships. We need to let the other know when something they've done has injured us. We can't expect our partner to change if he or she doesn't know there is a problem. None of us are mind readers, so start by being honest with yourself, articulate your frustration using *I* statements, and keep short accounts. It's much easier to work through one issue at a time, as they arise, rather than after months or even years of buildup.

Stay Committed

Disconnection happens. It is a normal part of the dance. Especially after the honeymoon (which lasts for about two and a half years[7]) has become a distant memory. Once we have settled in to a comfortable routine, it becomes easy not to attend to what is right in front of us—our partner. Remember the research mentioned in chapter 7—two-thirds of unhappy married couples end up being happy if they stick it out together.[8] Overcoming conflict is incredibly satisfying and draws us closer together, moving us from harmony to intimacy, but it requires us to be patient and hang in there, continually engaging and actively listening to our partner.

Remember the Big View . . . and Lean In!

Tim Keller writes that through marriage, the mystery of the gospel is unveiled. "The reason that marriage is so painful and yet wonderful is because it is a reflection of the gospel, which is painful and wonderful at once. . . . The hard times of marriage drive us to experience more of this transforming love of God. But a good marriage will also be a place where we experience more of this kind of transforming love at a human level."[9] When we are able to remember the big view—that marriage reveals something of eternal significance—the hope is that we will turn toward each other with our eyes, hearts, and minds set on restoration and intimacy and lean in to the challenge of loving each other as Christ has loved us.

Practice Forgiveness

"Then Peter came to Jesus and asked, 'Lord, how many times shall I forgive my brother or sister who sins against me? Up to seven times?' Jesus answered, 'I tell you, not seven times, but seventy-seven times'" (Matt. 18:21–22). Jesus knew we would frequently need to forgive each other because we are frequently wronged or hurt. Those we love the most, we will hurt the most. And those who love us will hurt us. It's par for the course. C. S. Lewis writes in *The Four Loves*:

Love anything, and your heart will certainly be wrung and possibly be broken. If you want to make sure of keeping it intact, you must give your heart to no one, not even to an animal. Wrap it carefully round with hobbies and little luxuries; avoid all entanglements; lock it up safe in the casket or coffin of your selfishness. But in that casket—safe, dark, motionless, airless—it will change. It will not be broken; it will become unbreakable, impenetrable, irredeemable.[10]

When we are hurt by others, it is our natural instinct to recoil in self-protection, yet we are called to "bear with each other and forgive one another if any of you has a grievance against someone," and to "forgive as the Lord forgave you" (Col. 3:13).

The Freedom of Forgiveness

This last and tenth point—forgiveness—is important enough to consider from multiple angles. Forgiveness is a choice; it's a conscious and intentional decision we make to let go of resentment or anger toward another person who has hurt us. It involves more than just letting go and moving on. True forgiveness goes a step further and offers compassion, understanding, and even empathy to the person who hurt us. When we truly forgive and have compassion we can say with Henri Nouwen:

In the face of the oppressed I recognize my own face and in the hands of the oppressor I recognize my own hands. Their flesh is my flesh; their blood is my blood, their pain is my pain; their smile is my smile. . . . There is nothing in me that does not belong to them, too. There is nothing in them that does not belong to me, too. In my heart, I know their yearning for love and down to my entrails, I can feel their cruelty. In another's eyes, I see my plea for forgiveness and in a hardened frown, I see my refusal. When someone murders, I know that I too could have murdered, and when someone gives birth, I know that I am capable of birth as well. In the depths of my being, I meet my fellow humans with whom I share love and hate, life and death.[11]

When we truly forgive, we recognize our common humanity—that we were all created from the same dust, capable of the same misgivings, subject to the same laws, and destined for the same end. Not only can we let go of the anger, hurt, and grievance that we had toward the other, but we can also move beyond and embrace him or her in love and compassion. In intimate relationships, the freeing power of forgiveness is transformative and breathes new life and joy into even the darkest corners of conflict.

★ *When we practice forgiveness we have more friends, longer marriages, and higher self-esteem.*

Better yet, when we choose to forgive—seventy times seven—we discover the command is in place for our own good, and we receive the reward of our forgiveness: freedom. We are free from toxic anger, resentment, tension, and stress. And we are free to live more joyfully. Research indicates that people who forgive have reduced anxiety and depression, better immune system function, fewer stress-related health issues, lower blood pressure, and lower mortality rates.[12] In cases of infidelity, research has shown that forgiveness is more important than time, relationship satisfaction, and commitment in overcoming the hurt and strengthening the relationship.[13] Not to mention that when we practice forgiveness we have more friends, longer marriages, and higher self-esteem, and we are more likely to be serene, hopeful, and agreeable.

Clearly, once again, Jesus knows what is best for us. He has shown us the ultimate example of forgiveness. He died on the cross for our sins, our ugliness, our wrongdoings. As Jesus told His disciples at the Last Supper, "This is my blood of the covenant, which is poured out for many for the forgiveness of sins" (Matt. 26:28). It is through Him that we have been forgiven and reconciled to God the Father. It is through Him that we have been wiped clean and presented as new. We don't deserve it; we could not have done it on our own. And yet we freely receive the gift of grace—that through Jesus's death we have been forgiven and set free.

So we are to forgive others. Jesus makes this very clear: "For if you forgive other people when they sin against you, your heavenly Father will also forgive you. But if you do not forgive others their sins, your

Father will not forgive your sins" (Matt. 6:14–15). Jesus is explicit in His command to forgive. It doesn't mean we forget the offense or condone or make excuses for the behavior; that's usually beyond our power. But it does mean that we release the other from blame, trusting God to be the ultimate, just judge. As Lewis Smedes wrote: "When you release the wrongdoer from the wrong, you cut a malignant tumor out of your inner life. You set a prisoner free, but you discover that the real prisoner was yourself."[14]

It is for freedom that Christ has set us free!

Summing Up
- Conflict is inevitable in relationships. Conflict without resolution leads merely to harmony; conflict with resolution leads to intimacy.
- When we sense a threat, our natural and automatic instinct is to protect ourselves. Stress hormones flood our system to prepare us to fight, flight, or freeze. Our amygdala takes over as our rational brain shuts down.
- In a heated argument with an intimate family member or partner, it's not unusual for us to respond with criticism, contempt, defensiveness, or stonewalling. These communication styles are known as the "four horsemen" and are detrimental to our relationships.
- It behooves us to learn skills to fight fairly, including techniques such as using *I* statements, claiming responsibility for our part, keeping short accounts, building appreciation, and practicing forgiveness.

So What?
Learning and practicing skills to engage in conflict effectively is key to successful, long-lasting, intimate relationships.

Conflict can bring two people closer together or can be a wedge that drives them apart over time. When we perceive a threat, our basic impulse is to protect ourselves by either fighting back, running away, or detaching; none of these are helpful. So we must learn new skills to fight well and fight fairly, knowing that conflict is a part of every relationship. And we must take Jesus's command to forgive seriously; it is essential to our mental and physical well-being!

Now What? Practical Applications
- Think through the way you handle conflict. What tends to be your general response—are you an avoider, actively ignoring and running away from conflict? Or do you subtly pretend like it doesn't exist? Do you meet it head-on and fight back? Do you stand your ground or quickly give in? Are you the peacemaker or negotiator in the family?
- Next time you are in a heated disagreement, take note of your physical and mental state. Consider the body language of your "opponent." Each of us has particular bodily and behavioral cues that serve as our alarm system, letting us know we feel threatened and our body is about to go on autopilot with our amygdala (emotional brain) taking over. It's at this point that you need to ground yourself in reality and remind yourself to relax and breathe slowly and rhythmically. If you're able to, dig deeper and ask yourself, "What is this really about?"
- Which of the horsemen (criticism, contempt, defensiveness, or stonewalling) is your go-to mode when facing conflict? Be honest and apply rigorous self-evaluation here. And then ask your significant other, spouse, best friend, or parent what they think. Ask siblings or other family members for their view of how conflict was and is modeled in your family.
- Next time you are in an argument, refrain from using any of the horsemen (and feel free to ask your partner to graciously keep you accountable).
- Use *I* statements when expressing your emotions and try to include your feeling, the observable behavior, and the effect it had on you. Here are some examples:
  - » "I'm annoyed (*feeling*) that you walked away from the table last night (*behavior*); it left me wondering if you really cared (*effect*) about what I had to say."
  - » "I feel anxious (*feeling and effect*) about your well-being when you don't text me back (*behavior*)."
- Practice conscious, nondefensive communication. During your next relational conflict, postpone your response by counting to ten, taking three breaths, and beginning your next sentence with, "I hear you

saying . . ." or, "It sounds like you . . ." Refrain from "Yes, but . . ." or cross-complaining.

- Practice using effective repair statements in your next conflict as a way to claim responsibility, build appreciation, and practice forgiveness. Here are some examples:
  - » I'm sorry; I messed up.
  - » Let me try again; I need a do-over.
  - » I can see my part in all of this.
  - » I overreacted. Please forgive me.
  - » I see your point, and it's a good one.
  - » Thank you for . . .
  - » I understand what you're saying—and it makes sense.
  - » One thing I appreciate about you is . . .
  - » I understand.
  - » I know that wasn't your intent.
  - » I didn't think that's what you meant, but that's how it felt.
  - » I forgive you.

Chapter Eleven

Play Together

"That was the best 'homework assignment' we've ever had, Dr. G.," James exuberantly exclaimed as he sat down on the couch.

Linea was quick to add, "We haven't laughed that hard together in a while. Clearly we should go out dancing more often."

"And not just any dancing—square dancing or line dancing it is. 'Do-si-do your partner, swing them round and round.'" James imitated the caller as he grinned from ear to ear. "You were so right when you said our marriage needed an extra dose of fun in it." He looked at me and softened his tone as he said, "Thank you."

James and Linea, not unlike many of the couples I work with, were in the "thick of it," or as they liked to call it—"the toilet seat up" stage. "Not only is the seat up, the door gets opened and we're caught with our pants down . . . often," Linea chuckled as she shared, but frustration and tears were close behind. "Between the kids, our careers, extended family, and all of the extras in life, we barely have time for ourselves, let alone each other. There just aren't enough hours in the day . . ." she said as her voice and shoulders dropped.

All Work and No Play

James and Linea are not alone in this balancing act. The number one stressor reported by Americans is not having enough time. Americans,

across all socioeconomic factors, are feeling stressed out! Marital interaction is declining,[1] workdays are longer, and leisure time is significantly
dropping. We spend less time on the basics—like sleeping and eating—
and time for play is vanishing from our schedules.[2] Between personal
and professional responsibilities—and the perception that play for adults
is unproductive, trivial, or even a guilty pleasure—we make no time to
play.

Play is not a human luxury, though. Monkeys and dogs and dolphins
and humans play. Since the beginning of time, and since our earliest years,
we play. No one teaches us; we just know how to play. Play is innate. And
it is a biological, social, and psychological necessity that is fundamental
to our health and well-being.[3] In other words, play matters for all of us.

✱ Be intentional about having fun together, face-to-face.

All too often, though, we think of play as being reserved for childhood, and somewhere between adolescence and adulthood we stop playing, despite our continued need for pleasure and novelty. For couples in
the "thick of it" stage of marriage, like James and Linea, the idea of having
time to play with each other seems inconceivable. In our fast-paced and
modern world, when we have downtime we're more likely to zone out in
front of a television, computer, or phone to catch the latest trends or check
out recent postings on our favorite social media sites. Playing on screens
has taken over a lot of our attention and free time today but doesn't count
as genuine play. Even if you're playing with someone else on a computer
screen, it doesn't have the same psychological benefits of free-flowing,
unstructured play that fosters creativity and laughter. Competitive games
where we have to "play by the rules" are also not the same as unregulated,
frivolous play. By definition, play is purposeless, fun, and all-consuming.[4]
It's important to note, however, that we don't need to follow the strict
definition of play to foster continued intimacy. The key is to be intentional about having fun together, face-to-face.

If you're single or dating, you might be reading this and thinking, "I
play all the time with my friends," or, "My boyfriend and I have a blast

together and often make time to play together." Perhaps you're recalling fun weekend trips, concerts, bike rides, hikes, and sweet times of simply hanging out. You're doing well and this chapter might not be as applicable to you—yet! File this away for the "thick of it" stage of life—and marriage in general. As responsibilities and stress increase, you might need to remind yourself and your partner how critical it is to laugh and play together.

Couples That Play Together Stay Together

The research is incredibly clear regarding the benefits of play. When couples play together—by engaging in new and fun activities—they grow closer to each other, report higher levels of marital satisfaction, and have better and longer-lasting relationships.[5] Studies show that sharing in new and exciting activities is consistently associated with better relationships as it keeps the relationship fresh. The more we invest in fun and friendship, the happier our marriage becomes over time.[6] Having fun together as a couple helps renew our marriage as we relate to our spouse in different ways by playing together.

Not only does playing together renew our marriage, it decreases our boredom. We all know boredom in marriage can be a killjoy, and if not addressed it can lead to marital dissatisfaction, the temptation to seek excitement outside of the relationship, or the all-too-common "we've just grown apart" reason for divorce.

Play helps us trust each other and feel safe.

Studies also show that when married couples make time to regularly hang out for fun, they improve their communication.[7] Think about the last time you were silly, uninhibited, or playful with your significant other. Maybe you played a game of chase, or what my family likes to call tickle monster, or a spontaneous game of keep-away. What happened afterward? Not only did you feel closer to each other, you often talked and giggled about the experience of playing together. Conversation is lighter and laughter comes more easily—enabling you to connect the good feelings experienced during the activity to the overall relationship. In essence, play builds up your reserves of positive communication and feelings about your partner and relationship.

Play helps us trust each other and feel safe. When we play together, our brain releases endorphins, our natural feel-good chemicals, and we create a positive bond with the other person.[8] When we share laughter and fun, not only do we feel better but we also feel closer to the person. And when we feel closer, we are more open to continued intimacy, more willing to resolve disagreements and conflict, and more likely to keep playing!

Back to the Basics: Reignite Your Inborn Playfulness

So how do we do it? How do we introduce or enhance playtime in our relationships? Let's start with a simple form of play that we all know how to do, and that is—flirting. Yes, *flirting*! Whether you are single or married—this is the starting point. There is a caveat, of course, for married folk—and that is, your flirting is to be done with your spouse. If you've got no strings attached, however, any eligible bachelor or bachelorette is fair game!

Why flirting, you wonder? Flirting comes naturally to all of us. We've done it—and been masters at it—since we were born. Flirting is a time-honored, universal, unspoken playful language used by men and women around the world. Not only is flirting good for our biological and psychological health[9] but it also has an incredible ripple effect and is a catalyst for increased play and humor in adult interactions. Flirting is a good-humored way to establish a connection and can be critical to maintaining a relationship over time—with benefits for both the flirt and the recipient! If you're the flirt, you will receive a boost in self-confidence and self-esteem. Dopamine—which is one of our feel-good chemicals—is released in our brains every time we playfully flirt with our partner. If you're the recipient, you also receive a boost—you feel desired, attractive, and special to your partner. It's a win-win.

In addition to your God-given gift of flirting, try some of these on for size to spice up your relationship:

- Go for a bike ride or a hike, or stand-up paddle together.
- Go out dancing (maybe try line or square dancing)!

- Travel and explore a new area.
- Plant and care for a garden together.
- Play chase or hide-and-seek.
- Dress up on a weeknight and eat leftovers by candlelight.
- Guess each other's favorite work in an art museum.
- Spend an evening getting crafty. If you have kids, break out the paint, coloring books, and modeling clay. If you don't have kids or easy access to craft supplies, go to a pottery or canvas-painting studio.
- Go to a park and play Frisbee, catch, or a pick-up game of soccer.

A little bit of play goes a long way in our relationships. Especially during the "thick of it" stage. Play and humor are "the soul's weapons in the fight for self-preservation . . . [and offer] an ability to rise above any situation, even if only for a few seconds."[10] Play enlivens us, energizes us, and renews us. It eases our burdens and reminds us to take ourselves less seriously. It promotes laughter and togetherness. It gives us an enthusiasm for life that is so vital. At a cosmic level, it's a reminder of our creative God, who gave us gushing springs, singing birds, chasing squirrels, and abundantly blossoming trees. What an amazing display of lavish divine activity!

So go ahead. Get going. Flirt often and play more.

The LORD wraps himself in light as with a garment;
    he stretches out the heavens like a tent
    and lays the beams of his upper chambers on their waters.
He makes the clouds his chariot
    and rides on the wings of the wind.
He makes winds his messengers. . . .

He makes springs pour water into the ravines;
    it flows between the mountains.
They give water to all the beasts of the field;
    the wild donkeys quench their thirst.
The birds of the sky nest by the waters;
    they sing among the branches. . . .

How many are your works, LORD!
  In wisdom you made them all;
  the earth is full of your creatures.
There is the sea, vast and spacious,
    teeming with creatures beyond number—
    living things both large and small.
There the ships go to and fro,
    and Leviathan, which you formed to frolic there.
                              (Ps. 104:2–4, 10–12, 24–26)

Summing Up

- Americans are more overworked than ever before; leisure time and family interaction is decreasing as more time is spent at work or in front of screens.
- Play—often viewed as unproductive for adults—is a universal, God-given gift to us that not only helps buffer stress but also fuels connection and intimacy in our relationships.
- Research is incredibly clear about numerous benefits of play for our marriages, including these:
  - » Increased marital satisfaction
  - » Longer-lasting relationships
  - » Improved communication

So What?

When we take the time to engage in fun, purposeless, playful activities with our spouse, our marriages are healthier and more intimate. It behooves us to be intentional with our time and make play a priority.

Given the number one stressor reported by Americans is not having enough time, we need to be mindful of ways in which we nurture our relationships. Playing together as a couple increases our marital satisfaction and communication, decreases potential boredom, and makes us feel good about our relationship and ourselves. We are designed by God to flourish through play at all ages and stages of life, and our marriages are enriched when we do so!

Now What? Practical Applications
- How do you think about play, specifically adulthood play? If you see it as something reserved for childhood, I challenge to you to consider its critical role and benefits during all stages of life.
- When was the last time you played with someone? Who was it and how did it come about? How did you feel afterward?
- If you are married, when was the last time you played with your spouse? How often do you engage in playful activities in your marriage? Has this changed over time?
- Reminisce about play-filled moments from childhood. What did you enjoy doing? How can you re-create that today?
- Make a list of things you like to do when you play. For example, it can be goofing around with your dog, reading aloud to your child, or dancing with your partner. Try to have at least seven things on your list. Have your partner do the same.
- Create a play jar using your collective ideas. Commit to having play-time with your partner as often as possible—at least once a week. Pull from the jar or freestyle it to see what playful activity you are doing together today!

Chapter Twelve

Maintain Curiosity

My first date with my husband was a total setup. Blind as blind can be. We went on foot to find a suitable restaurant. Suitable equals at least three occupied tables. Who knew there was an occupancy requirement for a first-date restaurant? I've come to realize since that it's a brilliant idea—none of us want to feel stuck in a quiet place with nothing to distract us from each other's awkward gaze on a first date. Occupancy wouldn't have mattered, though, for Thomas and me. We had plenty to talk about and conversation was easy, comfortable, and strangely familiar. He called me "sassy pants" before the night was over. Moments after our somewhat awkward goodbye, I remember telling my girlfriend, "I'm confident I will see him again."

And see him again I did. He called the next day, thanking *me* for such a lovely evening, followed by an invitation to join him at a dinner party the following weekend. And then beach walks, art shows, hikes, and concerts followed. Thomas always had a plan, and I felt pursued. He was intentional and sweet. (Note that our courtship predated the ubiquity of social media and dating apps!)

While my husband is still intentional and our love for each other deeper than ever, romantic beach walks have been replaced by taking turns at school drop-offs and lingering phone calls replaced with quick transactions about grocery lists. On good days, we are polite, kind, and thoughtful toward each other, but on our worst, we take each other for granted, get impatient, and are less tender toward each other.

So what happens long after the years of courtship are over? What happens when familiarity leads to complacency? How happy are the "ever after" years? Research indicates a dull disenchantment slowly begins to occur; the mundane facts of our partner's persona replace the idealized image we had, we become less motivated to impress our partner, and we stop putting our best foot forward.[1] In other words, life happens. Often our marriages get put on the back burner. The problem is, who signs up for a back-burner marriage?

Curiosity: Fatal for the Cat but Essential for the Couple

One seemingly simple way to help make our marriage a priority is to remain curious. There is an increasing amount of research that suggests curiosity may play a central role in our relationships. Defined broadly as "a strong desire to know or learn something,"[2] curiosity has often been associated with learning, creativity, and intellectual engagement. Recent studies are finding that when we are curious, we are more socially connected, seen as more attractive, and we engage in more intimate conversations. Think about it—when we are open and interested, we are more likely to listen, ask questions, and foster depth and intimacy in our relationships.[3] This is true across the board—with friends, family members, and romantic relationships. Curious people are happier, healthier, and more empathetic.[4] Additionally, curiosity protects us from rejection and helps us navigate hard times. For example, if your boyfriend or girlfriend breaks up with you, or your spouse is "not in the mood" to be intimate on a certain night, and you assume a stance of curiosity—wondering what's going on with them or the situation—instead of immediately jumping to the conclusion *I must have done something wrong*, both acceptance and understanding are increased. The research is clear: curiosity benefits us not just intellectually but psychologically and relationally as well.

Curiosity is also a key component of mindfulness—the act of bringing one's attention and awareness to experiences occurring in the present moment. Mindfulness, rooted in many spiritual traditions, including the Christian faith, has become a hot topic in the field of psychology. Numerous studies speak to its effectiveness in treating anxiety and everyday stressors. Research indicates that being curious and mindful—inquiring about the entirety of our experience, whether pleasant or unpleasant—is helpful in our intimate relationships, especially when disagreements and conflicts arise.[5] When we are curious and mindful, we are more likely to have the capacity to approach rather than avoid pain, ground ourselves in the present rather than worry about what's next, practice kindness rather than judgment, and remain receptive rather than closed off.

Jesus embodies mindfulness. He teaches us—through His words and actions—to be aware and watchful, to remain open and investigative. Perhaps an extreme example, but one of my favorites, is His posture during the Last Supper: fully present in the face of impending death. On the night Jesus was betrayed, He took bread, broke it, and said, "Take and eat; this is my body" (Matt. 26:26). Then He took a cup and gave it to His disciples, saying, "Drink from it, all of you. This is my blood of the covenant, which is poured out for many for the forgiveness of sins" (vv. 27–28). Talk about being present and having the ability to approach rather than avoid pain! Jesus is the ultimate example of mindfulness. If only we could remain that attentive and kind in our relationships.

✶✶✶ Curious people are happier, healthier, and more empathetic.

Comfort leads to complacency or, as one husband put it, "There are no more surprises between us; we know each other so well." Some couples might say they know almost everything about their spouse—they can predict what will be said next, how the other is feeling at a particular gathering, or what their spouse's reaction would be to an idea. There's nothing inherently wrong with intimately knowing our spouse! We should have a sense of the other—their thoughts, feelings, and reactions. This is what helps us feel known and loved. At the same time, we need to be careful of assuming we know it all. When we think we know everything, we stop asking, and we have a tendency to stop listening. We become distracted and dismissive at times, not taking interest in our partner's life. When mutual curiosity is lost, our relationship suffers.

The reality is—there is always more to learn. Whether you've been married for fifteen years or fifteen days, there is something new to discover. We all evolve and change over time. Couples who make an effort to remain interested in each other's daily occurrences report feeling closer and more cared for. One of my clients put it best when she turned to her husband of five years and said, "When you take the time to ask me how my day was—to check in and hear about my world of diapers, spit-up, and nap demons—I feel cared for and important. It's a simple way for you to let me know that I matter."

Twenty Questions

The first step in cultivating curiosity is to recognize that your assumptions hinder you from approaching your partner with an open mindset. If you think you already know it all, think again! Be aware of thoughts that prevent you from taking a sincere interest in your partner. Thoughts such as *She's an open book and I've read every page* or *He's a simple guy; I've got him figured out.* Challenge those assumptions as you contemplate the complexity of the human being.

Take an active interest in the other, spending time getting to know them, asking open-ended questions, and listening attentively.

The next step is where it gets fun. If you are married, pretend like you are dating and treat each other accordingly. (Of course, if you are single and dating, this will be easy!) For those who can hardly remember the dating days—let me remind you of what often occurs during courtships. We take an active interest in the other, spending time getting to know them, asking open-ended questions, and listening attentively. We put our best foot forward, wanting to engage on an increasingly deeper level. We remain open and interested.

Researcher John Gottman coined the term "love maps."[6] This is the place where we store important and relevant information about our partner—memories from their past, details of the present, and hopes for the future. Our deepest fears and often unspoken, grandest dreams are included in our love maps. Think of it as a sketch of your partner's inner world—a map that continues to evolve and change over time as a result of significant relationships and experiences. It is within our relationships that we have the opportunity—*if* we remain curious—to build our love maps and come to a deeper understanding of and appreciation for our partner.

The first step of building your love map occurs on your own. Think through your story—the significant people, challenges, triumphs, and events—and what has brought you to this place, shaping and sharpening you along the way. (If you answered the questions posed throughout the first part of this book, "What's Your Once Upon a Time?" you have a serious jump start!) Now think about enhancing your love map with your partner. Write down ten questions to ask your partner, and have your partner do the same; they can be silly and playful or more serious and challenging. Some examples would be:

- What is your least favorite food?
- What were you wearing the night of our first date?
- What is one of your most embarrassing moments?
- If you could change one thing about yourself, what would it be?
- What is one of your biggest regrets in life?

Compile your list of questions and take turns asking and answering each question, listening attentively when your partner shares. Even if you think you already know what your partner will say, it's the process of asking and responding that allows for deepening emotional intimacy.[7]

The Joy of Discovery

In all our relationships, it behooves us to maintain curiosity. Let us not assume we know it all, but rather let's take time each day to discover something new about the other or be reminded of something we appreciate. Make an effort, like you seamlessly did in the early days of your relationship, to take an interest in your partner. Both the big and small things. The mundane and significant. Simply acknowledging and responding to your partner builds connections. It lets them know you care. It is in these moments of interest and curiosity that we foster love, passion, and connection.

Summing Up

- When we have known someone for a while, it is easy to settle in to a routine and become complacent in our relationship. Familiarity and comfort can breed inattentiveness and disinterest.
- Remaining open and curious in our committed relationships leads to increased connectedness, greater empathy, and more resilience.
- Specific practices and exercises, such as taking the posture of a listener, letting go of preconceived notions, practicing mindfulness, and asking open-ended questions, can help build curiosity in a relationship and lead to greater intimacy.

So What?

When we take an active interest in our partner—remaining curious and open—intimacy and connection deepen.

It is easy to take our partner for granted after years of being together. Assumptions, indifference, and disenchantment set in, and we think we know it all. We would be wise to renounce the illusion of omniscience and adopt a posture of curiosity. Our relationships will reap the benefits as we seek to continually deepen our understanding and love for each other.

Now What? Practical Applications

- Think about one of your intimate relationships. What assumptions do you bring to the table about the other person? Do you feel like you know them so well you can predict their reactions and thoughts? If so, how might this impact the way you relate to each other? Discuss the ways this level of familiarity has been either helpful or harmful in your relationship.
- Find out one new thing about your partner today. This needs to be initiated by *you* asking a question, whether it's about a current or past event or story. Take turns.
- Alternatively, share with your partner one thing they may not know about you. Again, take turns with this exercise.

- Commit to showing interest in your partner in one particular area that you know would mean a lot to him or her. Maintain this curiosity for the upcoming month.
- Sometime in the next two weeks, buy and play one of the "get-to-know-you" board or card games with your partner or someone you are intimate with. Some examples are The Ungame (couples version), Apples to Apples, and Boxers or Briefs?
- Practice mindfulness, even when it's most difficult such as during conflict, under stress, or at the end of a long day. Do this by grounding yourself in the present moment—being fully aware of your thoughts, feelings, and physiological reactions. For example, if during a conversation you are triggered by a comment your partner makes, instead of reflexively responding, walking away, or going silent, take a deep breath and say, "I just noticed my stomach knotted up when you said that—give me a second to process. I need to gather my thoughts."
- Purchase and play the Gottman love maps game found here: https://www.gottman.com/product/love-map-card-decks/.

Reclaiming the Story of Love

When Sharon and Steve walked into my office for their first counseling session, they could barely make eye contact, let alone sit next to each other on the couch. Three years of a bumpy marriage and they were ready to throw in the towel. After many months of intensively working together, the picture looked entirely different.

"Dr. Gurney, we are so grateful for the ways you've helped us reconnect with each other," Sharon said. "I really didn't think we'd make it. Our families can't believe the difference in our marriage—or that we're even still together."

Steve added, "Not only is our marriage in a better place, I feel better equipped in general. My communication at work, with my parents, and even my own self-talk is so much healthier."

"You two deserve all the credit," I replied. "You've done the hard work of digging deep, and it has truly been a privilege to be part of the process. Thank you for allowing me to walk with you in this—even going into some of the darker and harder places of your past."

Over the years I've seen hundreds of individuals, families, and couples like Sharon and Steve face their relational challenges, fears, and inadequacies head-on. Some situations are more complicated than others and not all resolve quickly or well, but there is always hope for healing, growth, and redemption. I wouldn't be in this field if I didn't believe that to be true.

Through this book we've explored numerous relational topics, consulted research, visited some of my clients and students, dissected relational challenges, and debunked myths. Wisdom from Scripture has been highlighted and practical next steps offered. Everything points to the fact that although we are hardwired to seek connection and love, we have trouble doing relationships well. Relational intimacy in our families, marriages, society, and institutions is missing the mark.

The real takeaway from our exploration of relationships is this—healthy, loving, and long-lasting relationships *are* possible but don't come without the difficult work of understanding ourselves and changing our behaviors. They require that we let go of the fairy tale, engage in self-examination and skill building, and apply generous doses of grace to ourselves and others.

So it is time. It's time to reclaim our relational birthright. It's time to renounce the illusion of the autonomous self and accept belonging. From dust we all come, and to dust we will return; and in the in-between, we must embrace the complexities of our humanity and learn to love boldly and love well in this thing called life. This is, after all, the message we have heard from the beginning—that we are to love one another (1 John 3:11). Loving relationships and intimate connections ensure our existence. Will you join me as we reclaim this story of love?

Acknowledgments

They say it takes a village to raise a child. I say it takes a village to write a book. And I am so grateful for the people in my village.

Thank you, Little Red—aka Kathleen Matthews—for believing not only in this book but also in my ability to write it. You have encouraged, challenged, sharpened, and supported me every step of the way. From inception to final edits, your wisdom and insight are found in the pages within. Thank you, friend, for your presence in my life. What a gift to have you as a soul sister and to know you're the guardian for my girls. Twenty-five years of adventures together and my days are truly richer and fuller because of you. I love you, friend.

For my urban tribe, whether from Boston days or Santa Barbara, doing life alongside you is a gift. Thank you for being part of my journey. Rainbow T (aka Lisa Desrochers)—your steadfast friendship and listening ear bring comfort to my soul.

To Keely Boeving—my agent. Your belief in this book and its purpose helped me believe in it. Thank you for your keen eye and insights. And thanks to the entire team at Kregel Publications; your talent and discernment are deeply appreciated.

For my energetic, fun-loving, and inspiring Westmont College students! Your curiosity, eagerness, genuine care, and goodwill are simply some of the things I love about you all. (Not to mention the fact that you try to help me stay hip and give me great material for dating blogs!) Teaching and learning alongside you is such a gift. A specific shout-out to my research assistants, Megan Fuller and Cameron Haramia—you were there when this book project began and have been my number one fans since. Anna Vandebunte and Branon Eusebio—you guys helped me take it to the next level and your enthusiasm was my fuel. And Kendall Songer—your steadfast and solid work in the final stages helped keep me sane. Thank you.

To all my clients who shared your stories with me—the hard and painful ones: thank you. You have allowed me to enter your lives, trusting me with the intimate, the shameful, and the sacred. What a gift it is to walk alongside you on this journey as fellow sojourners, reminding one another that we are all broken and cracked, and yet it is through the cracks we see the light. This book would not be without you.

To Dad, Barbara, Melissa, and Pete—I am thankful you are a part of my life! There are more adventures, laughter, and love because of your presence.

To Goof and Mamolas—you have shaped and grown me in ways that I am still learning about. You have helped make me strong, taught me to never give up, and loved me despite my stubbornness. Thank you, Mamolas, for believing that I hung the moon. And Goof, thank you for hanging the moon in so many ways in my eyes; you're an inspiring big sis. I am so grateful to be a Gurney Girl.

And to my family, I am indebted. Thomas, my traveling partner and love—your gentle and wise insights, encouragement, and support have helped make this dream a reality. Sweet Kate—from the day you were born you stole my heart. Madeline—your curiosity, passion, and transparency make my heart smile. You three have taught me how to love bigger and better.

And to God the Father, God the Son, and God the Holy Spirit—my refuge and strength.

Further Reading

Chapter One: Wired for Love
Attachment and Loss, vol. 1, John Bowlby
Attachment in Adulthood, Mario Mikulincer and Phillip R. Shaver
"Attachment Styles and Close Relationships," quiz designed by R. Chris Fraley,
   PhD (http://www.web-research-design.net/cgi-bin/crq/crq.pl)
Becoming Attached, Robert Karen
Hold Me Tight, Sue Johnson
How We Love, Milan and Kay Yerkovich
Your God Is Too Small, J. B. Phillips

Chapter Two: Monkey See, Monkey Do
Knowing God, J. I. Packer
Social Foundations of Thought and Action, Albert Bandura
Social Learning Theory, Albert Bandura

Chapter Three: Mirror, Mirror, on the Wall
Emotional Intelligence, Daniel Goleman
Mindset, Carol Dweck
Self-Efficacy, Albert Bandura
The Developing Mind, Daniel Siegel

Chapter Four: It All Goes Back to the Toy Box
A Sword Between the Sexes?, Mary Stewart Van Leeuwen
After Eden, Mary Stewart Van Leeuwen

Discovering Biblical Equality, Ronald W. Pierce and Rebecca Merrill Groothuis
"Gender and Emotion: Theory, Findings, and Context," Leslie R. Brody, Judith
    A. Hall, and Lynissa R. Stokes, in *Handbook of Emotions*, 4th ed., edited
    by Lisa Feldman Barrett, Michael Lewis, and Jeannette Haviland-Jones.
Gender and Grace, Mary Stewart Van Leeuwen
Man and Woman, One in Christ, Philip Barton Payne
Neither Complementarian nor Egalitarian, Michelle Lee-Barnewall
Paul and Gender, Cynthia Long Westfall
Paul, Women, and Wives, Craig S. Keener
"The Bible Teaches the Equal Standing of Man and Woman," Philip Barton Payne
    (https://www.pbpayne.com/wp-content/uploads/2015/07/Payne.pdf)
"The Gender Similarities Hypothesis," Janet Shibley Hyde (https://www.apa
    .org/pubs/journals/releases/amp-606581.pdf)

Chapter Five: Anchoring in Rough Seas
"Emerging Adulthood," Jeffrey Jensen Arnett (http://www.jeffreyarnett.com
    /articles/ARNETT_Emerging_Adulthood_theory.pdf)
Report of the APA Task Force on the Sexualization of Girls, Eileen L. Zurbrig-
    gen, Rebecca L. Collins, Sharon Lamb, Tomi-Ann Roberts, Deborah L.
    Tolman, L. Monique Ward, and Jeanne Blake (https://www.apa.org/pi
    /women/programs/girls/report-full.pdf)
So Sexy So Soon, Diane E. Levin and Jean Kilbourne
The Defining Decade, Meg Jay

Chapter Six: Someday My Prince Will Come
"Birds of a Feather Do Flock Together," Wu Youyou, David Stillwell, H.
    Andrew Schwartz, and Michal Kosinski (http://journals.sagepub.com/doi
    /pdf/10.1177/0956797616678187)
Love Sense, Sue Johnson
Playing and Reality, Donald W. Winnicott
The Soul Mate Myth, Jean Cirillo

Chapter Seven: You Had Me at Hello
Hold Me Tight, Sue Johnson
This Momentary Marriage, John Piper

Chapter Eight: *Later, at the Castle*
The Meaning of Marriage, Timothy Keller
The Seven Principles for Making Marriage Work, John Gottman and Nan Silver

Chapter Nine: *Speak the Truth*
The Dance of Connection, Harriet Lerner
The Five Love Languages, Gary Chapman

Chapter Ten: *Fight Fair and Forgive Often*
Forgive and Forget, Lewis B. Smedes
Forgiveness and Health, Loren Toussaint, Everett Worthington, and David R.
    Williams
The Peacemaker, Ken Sande

Chapter Eleven: *Play Together*
Play, Stuart Brown
The Overworked American, Juliet Schor

Chapter Twelve: *Maintain Curiosity*
"Love Maps," John Gottman (https://www.integralpsychology.org/uploads/1/5/3
    /0/15300482/wkbk_2.pdf)
"The Sound Relationship House," Ellie Lisitsa (https://www.gottman.com/blog
    /the-sound-relationship-house-build-love-maps/)

Notes

Chapter One: Wired for Love

1. Sue Johnson, *Love Sense: The Revolutionary New Science of Romantic Relationships* (New York: Little, Brown, 2013), 18–19.
2. John Bowlby, *Attachment and Loss* (New York: Basic Books, 1983), 27.
3. Debra Umberson and Jennifer Karas Montez, "Social Relationships and Health: A Flashpoint for Health Policy," *Journal of Health and Social Behavior* 51 (2010): 54–66.
4. T. F. Robles and J. K. Kiecolt-Glaser, "The Physiology of Marriage: Pathways to Health," *Physiology and Behavior* 79, no. 3 (2003): 409–16.
5. Shamai Davidson, "Human Reciprocity Among the Jewish Prisoners in the Nazi Concentration Camps," in *The Nazi Concentration Camps* (Jerusalem: Yad Vashem, 1984): 555–72, http://www.yadvashem.org/odot _pdf/Microsoft%20Word%20-%203554.pdf.
6. Lex L. Merrill et al., "Predicting the Impact of Child Sexual Abuse on Women: The Role of Abuse Severity, Parental Support, and Coping Strategies," *Journal of Consulting and Clinical Psychology* 69, no. 6 (2001): 992–1006.
7. Johnson, *Love Sense*, 19.
8. C. S. Lewis, *Mere Christianity* (New York: HarperOne, 2015), 175.
9. Mary D. Salter Ainsworth et al., *Patterns of Attachment: A Psychological Study of the Strange Situation* (Hillsdale, NJ: Erlbaum, 1978), 32.
10. These questions are adapted from the unpublished work *Adult Attachment Interview (AAI) Protocol* excerpted from George, Kaplan, and Main (1996) and were designed to get at the level of loving attachment that adults had during their own childhood. See Erik Hesse, "The Adult

Attachment Interview: Protocol, Method of Analysis, and Empirical Studies: 1985–2015," in *Handbook of Attachment: Theory, Research, and Clinical Applications*, 3rd ed., ed. Jude Cassidy and Phillip R. Shaver (New York: Guilford, 2016), 553–97.

11. Mary Main and Judith Solomon, "Discovery of an Insecure-Disorganized/ Disoriented Attachment Pattern," in *Affective Development in Infancy*, ed. Michael Yogman and T. Berry Brazelton (Norwood, NJ: Ablex, 1986), 95–124.

Chapter Two: Monkey See, Monkey Do

1. Albert Bandura, Dorothea Ross, and Sheila A. Ross, "Transmission of Aggression Through Imitation of Aggressive Models," *Journal of Abnormal and Social Psychology* 63, no. 3 (1961): 575–82.

2. Douglas A. Gentile, Sarah Coyne, and David A. Walsh, "Media Violence, Physical Aggression, and Relational Aggression in School Age Children: A Short-Term Longitudinal Study," *Aggressive Behavior* 37, no. 2 (2011): 193–206.

3. Günnur Karakurt, Margaret Keiley, and German Posada, "Intimate Relationship Aggression in College Couples: Family-of-Origin Violence, Egalitarian Attitude, Attachment Security," *Journal of Family Violence* 28, no. 6 (2013): 561–75.

4. Amanda Sheffield Morris et al., "The Influence of Mother-Child Emotion Regulation Strategies on Children's Expression of Anger and Sadness," *Developmental Psychology* 47, no. 1 (2011): 213–25.

5. Ashley L. Hill et al., "Profiles of Externalizing Behavior Problems for Boys and Girls Across Preschool: The Roles of Emotion Regulation and Inattention," *Developmental Psychology* 42, no. 5 (2006): 913–28.

Chapter Three: Mirror, Mirror, on the Wall

1. Daniel J. Siegel, *Mindsight: The New Science of Personal Transformation* (New York: Bantam, 2010), 59.

2. Rick van Baaren et al., "Where Is the Love? The Social Aspects of Mimicry," *Philosophical Transactions of the Royal Society B: Biological Sciences* 364, no. 1528 (2009): 2383.

3. Edward Tronick et al., "The Infant's Response to Entrapment Between

Contradictory Messages in Face-to-Face Interaction," *Journal of the American Academy of Child and Adolescent Psychiatry* 17, no. 1 (1978): 1–13.

4. Daniel J. Siegel and Tina Payne Bryson, *The Whole-Brain Child: 12 Revolutionary Strategies to Nurture Your Child's Developing Mind* (New York: Bantam, 2012), 122.

5. Laura E. Berk, *Child Development*, 9th ed. (New York: Pearson, 2012), 399.

6. L. Alan Sroufe, *Emotional Development: The Organization of Emotional Life in the Early Years* (Cambridge: Cambridge University Press, 1995), 44–45.

7. Berk, *Child Development*, 409.

8. Carol S. Dweck, *Mindset: The New Psychology of Success* (New York: Ballantine Books, 2016), 6–7.

9. Dweck, *Mindset*, 12.

10. Dana A. Weiser and Daniel J. Weigel, "Self-Efficacy in Romantic Relationships: Direct and Indirect Effects on Relationship Maintenance and Satisfaction," *Personality and Individual Differences* 89 (2016): 152–56.

Chapter Four: It All Goes Back to the Toy Box

1. May Ling Halim and Diane Ruble, "Gender Identity and Stereotyping in Early and Middle Childhood," in *Handbook of Gender Research in Psychology: Gender Research in General and Experimental Psychology*, vol. 1, ed. Joan C. Chrisler and Donald R. McCreary (New York: Springer, 2010), 495–525.

2. Melissa W. Clearfield and Naree M. Nelson, "Sex Differences in Mothers' Speech and Play Behavior with 6-, 9-, and 14-Month-Old Infants," *Sex Roles* 54, nos. 1–2 (2006): 127–37.

3. Jean Berko Gleason and Richard Ely, "Gender Differences in Language Development," in *Biology, Society, and Behavior: The Development of Sex Differences in Cognition*, ed. Ann McGillicuddy-De Lisi and Richard De Lisi (Westport, CT: Ablex, 2002), 127–40.

4. Clearfield and Nelson, "Sex Differences in Mothers' Speech and Play Behavior," 129.

5. Adrian Furnham, Emma Reeves, and Salima Budhani, "Parents Think Their Sons Are Brighter Than Their Daughters: Sex Differences in

Parental Self-Estimation and Estimations of Their Children's Multiple Intelligences," *Journal of Genetic Psychology* 163, no. 1 (2002): 24–39.

6. Leslie R. Brody, Judith A. Hall, and Lynissa R. Stokes, "Gender and Emotion: Theory, Findings, and Context," in *Handbook of Emotions*, 4th ed., ed. Lisa Feldman Barrett, Michael Lewis, and Jeannette Haviland-Jones (New York: Guilford, 2016), 384.

7. Robyn Beaman, Kevin Wheldall, and Coral Kemp, "Differential Teacher Attention to Boys and Girls in the Classroom," *Educational Review* 58, no. 3 (2006): 339–66.

8. Carol J. Auster and Claire S. Mansbach, "The Gender Marketing of Toys: An Analysis of Color and Type of Toy on the Disney Store Website," *Sex Roles* 67, nos. 7–8 (2012): 375–88.

9. Lin Bian, Sarah-Jane Leslie, and Andrei Cimpian, "Gender Stereotypes About Intellectual Ability Emerge Early and Influence Children's Interests," *Science* 355, no. 6323 (2017): 389–91.

10. Vasanti Jadva, Melissa Hines, and Susan Golombok, "Infants' Preferences for Toys, Colors, and Shapes: Sex Differences and Similarities," *Archives of Sexual Behavior* 39, no. 6 (2010): 1261–73.

11. Franzis Preckel et al., "Gender Differences in Gifted and Average-Ability Students: Comparing Girls' and Boys' Achievement, Self-Concept, Interest, and Motivation in Mathematics," *Gifted Child Quarterly* 52, no. 2 (2008): 146–59.

12. Janet Shibley Hyde, "The Gender Similarities Hypothesis," *American Psychologist* 60, no. 6 (2005): 581–92. Hyde grouped gender differences into six broad categories: cognitive variables, verbal and nonverbal communication, social and personality variables (i.e., aggression or leadership), psychological well-being (i.e., self-esteem), motor behavior, and miscellaneous constructs (i.e., moral reasoning). Only a few main differences appeared: compared with women, men could throw farther, were more physically aggressive, masturbated more, and had more positive attitudes about sex in an uncommitted relationship.

13. Philip B. Payne, "The Bible Teaches the Equal Standing of Man and Woman," *Priscilla Papers* 29, no. 1 (2015): https://www.cbeinternational.org/resources/article/priscilla-papers/bible-teaches-equal-standing-man-and-woman.

Chapter Five: Anchoring in Rough Seas

1. Malcolm P. Young et al., "Analysis of Connectivity: Neural Systems in the Cerebral Cortex," *Reviews in the Neurosciences* 5, no. 3 (1994): 227–50.

2. Jeffrey Jensen Arnett and Joseph Schwab, *The Clark University Poll of Emerging Adults: Thriving, Struggling, and Hopeful* (Worcester, MA: Clark University, 2012), 7, https://www2.clarku.edu/clark-poll-emerging-adults /pdfs/clark-university-poll-emerging-adults-findings.pdf.

3. Eileen L. Zurbriggen et al., *Report of the APA Task Force on the Sexualization of Girls* (Washington, DC: American Psychological Association, 2007), 1–2, http://www.apa.org/pi/women/programs/girls/report-full.pdf.

4. Barbara L. Frederickson et al., "That Swimsuit Becomes You: Sex Differences in Self-Objectification, Restrained Eating, and Math Performance," *Journal of Personality and Social Psychology* 75, no. 1 (1998): 269–84.

5. Barbara L. Frederickson and Kristen Harrison, "Throwing Like a Girl: Self-Objectification Predicts Adolescent Girls' Motor Performance," *Journal of Sport and Social Issues* 29, no. 1 (2005): 79–101.

6. Zurbriggen, *Report of the APA Task Force on the Sexualization of Girls*, 2.

7. Deborah Schooler and L. Monique Ward, "Average Joes: Men's Relationships with Media, Real Bodies, and Sexuality," *Psychology of Men and Masculinity* 7, no. 1 (2006): 27–41.

8. Carolyn C. Ross, "Overexposed and Under-Prepared: The Effects of Early Exposure to Sexual Content," *Psychology Today*, August 13, 2012, https:// www.psychologytoday.com/blog/real-healing/201208/overexposed-and -under-prepared-the-effects-early-exposure-sexual-content.

9. Kimberly R. Johnson and Bjarne M. Holmes, "Contradictory Messages: A Content Analysis of Hollywood-Produced Romantic Comedy Feature Films," *Communication Quarterly* 57, no. 3 (2009): 352–73.

10. Litsa Renée Tanner et al., "Images of Couples and Families in Disney Feature-Length Animated Films," *American Journal of Family Therapy* 31, no. 5 (2003): 355–73.

11. Christine M. Bachen and Eva Illouz, "Imagining Romance: Young People's Cultural Models of Romance and Love," *Critical Studies in Mass Communication* 13, no. 4 (1996): 279–308.

12. Chris Segrin and Robin L. Nabi, "Does Television Viewing Cultivate

Unrealistic Expectations About Marriage?" *Journal of Communication* 52, no. 2 (2002): 247–63.

Chapter Six: Someday My Prince Will Come

1. Barbara Dafoe Whitehead and David Popenoe, "The State of Our Unions: The Social Health of Marriage in America 2003," *Theology Matters* 10, no. 2 (2004): 3, http://www.theologymatters.com/MarApr04.pdf.

2. Bjarne M. Holmes, "In Search of My 'One-and-Only': Romance-Oriented Media and Beliefs in Romantic Relationship Destiny," *Electronic Journal of Communication* 17, nos. 3–4 (2007), http://www.cios.org/EJCPUBLIC/017/3/01735.HTML.

3. Shankar Vedantam, "Social Isolation Growing in U.S., Study Says," *Washington Post*, June 23, 2006, http://www.washingtonpost.com/wp-dyn/content/article/2006/06/22/AR2006062201763.html.

4. Robert D. Putnam, *Bowling Alone: The Collapse and Revival of American Community* (New York: Simon and Schuster, 2000), 57–58.

5. C. Raymond Knee, "Implicit Theories of Relationships: Assessment and Prediction of Romantic Relationship Initiation, Coping, and Longevity," *Journal of Personality and Social Psychology* 74, no. 2 (1998), 360–70.

6. C. Raymond Knee and Kristen N. Petty, "Implicit Theories of Relationships: Destiny and Growth Beliefs," in *The Oxford Handbook of Close Relationships*, ed. Jeffry A. Simpson and Lorne Campbell (New York: Oxford University Press, 2013), 183–98.

7. Vanessa Van Edwards, "The Science of Soulmates," *HuffPost*, December 6, 2017, http://www.huffingtonpost.com/vanessa-van-edwards/the-science-of-soulmates_b_9073590.html.

8. Paul W. Eastwick and Eli J. Finkel, "Sex Differences in Mate Preferences Revisited: Do People Know What They Initially Desire in a Romantic Partner?," *Journal of Personality and Social Psychology* 94, no. 2 (2008): 245–64.

9. Donald Woods Winnicott, *Playing and Reality* (New York: Routledge, 1971), 193.

Chapter Seven: You Had Me at Hello

1. Darren K. Carlson, "Over Half of Americans Believe in Love at First

Sight," Gallup, February 14, 2001, http://www.gallup.com/poll/2017/over
-half-americans-believe-love-first-sight.aspx.

2. Health eNews, "Men Fall in Love Faster Than Women, Study Finds,"
February 12, 2016, http://www.ahchealthenews.com/2016/02/12/do-you
-believe-in-love-at-first-sight/.

3. *Merriam-Webster Online*, s.v. "lust," accessed January 7, 2019, https://
www.merriam-webster.com/dictionary/lust.

4. Urban Dictionary, s.v. "lust," accessed January 7, 2019, https://www
.urbandictionary.com/define.php?term=lust.

5. Helen E. Fisher et al., "Defining the Brain Systems of Lust, Romantic
Attraction, and Attachment," *Archives of Sexual Behavior* 31, no. 5 (2002):
413–19.

6. Helen Fisher, "Anthropologist and Love Expert Helen Fisher on the
Mysteries of Love," interview by David Levine, Elsevier, July 29, 2014,
https://www.elsevier.com/connect/anthropologist-and-love-expert-helen
-fisher-on-the-mysteries-of-love.

7. Fisher, "Helen Fisher on the Mysteries of Love."

8. Margery Williams, *The Velveteen Rabbit* (New York: Delacorte Press,
1958), 5.

9. James Coan, Hillary Schaefer, and Richard J. Davidson, "Lending a
Hand: Social Regulation of the Neural Response to Threat," *Psychological
Science* 17, no. 12 (2007): 1032–39.

10. "Attraction Can Grow with Time Spent Together," HealthDay, July 6,
2015, https://consumer.healthday.com/pregnancy-information-29/love
-sex-and-relationship-health-news-452/attraction-can-grow-with-time
-spent-together-700903.html.

11. Linda J. Waite et al., *Does Divorce Make People Happy? Findings from a
Study of Unhappy Marriages* (New York: Institute for American Values,
2002), http://americanvalues.org/catalog/pdfs/does_divorce_make_peo
ple_happy.pdf.

Chapter Eight: Later, at the Castle

1. "Marriage and Divorce," American Psychological Association, accessed
March 26, 2018, http://www.apa.org/topics/divorce/.

2. Christine Gross-Loh, "The First Lesson of Marriage 101: There Are No

Soul Mates," *Atlantic*, February 12, 2014, https://www.theatlantic.com /education/archive/2014/02/the-first-lesson-of-marriage-101-there-are -no-soul-mates/283712/.

3. Paul R. Amato and Denise Previti, "People's Reasons for Divorcing: Gender, Social Class, the Life Course, and Adjustment," *Journal of Family Issues* 24, no. 5 (2003): 602–26.

4. Xenia P. Montenegro, *The Divorce Experience: A Study of Divorce at Midlife and Beyond* (Washington, DC: AARP, 2004), https://assets.aarp .org/rgcenter/general/divorce.pdf.

5. Ted L. Huston, "What's Love Got to Do with It? Why Some Marriages Succeed and Others Fail," *Personal Relationships* 16, no. 3 (2009): 301–27.

6. Eric Barker, "How to Live Happily Ever After, According to Science," *The Week*, May 6, 2014, http://theweek.com/articles/447400/how-live-happily -ever-after-according-science.

7. C. S. Lewis, *Mere Christianity* (New York: HarperOne, 2015), 138.

8. Timothy Keller, *The Meaning of Marriage: Facing the Complexities of Commitment with the Wisdom of God* (New York: Penguin, 2011), 119–46.

9. Wendy Strgar, "Love that Works: A Philosophy for Lasting Relationships," *HuffPost*, November 17, 2011, http://www.huffingtonpost.com/wendy -strgar/love-love-that-works-a-ph_b_593553.html.

10. Eric Barker, "Can You Improve Your Relationship by Trying to Change Your Partner?," *Barking Up the Wrong Tree* (blog), accessed January 7, 2019, http://www.bakadesuyo.com/2011/04/can-you-improve-your-relation ship-by-trying-t/.

11. John M. Gottman and Nan Silver, *The Seven Principles for Making Marriage Work* (New York: Harmony, 1999), 130.

12. Ted L. Huston and Renate M. Houts, "The Psychological Infrastructure of Courtship and Marriage: The Role of Personality and Compatibility in Romantic Relationships," in *The Developmental Course of Marital Dysfunction*, ed. Thomas N. Bradbury (Cambridge: Cambridge University Press, 1998), 114–51.

Chapter Nine: Speak the Truth

1. Saul McLeod, "Asch Experiment," Simply Psychology, 2008, https://www .simplypsychology.org/asch-conformity.html.

2. Timothy Keller, *The Meaning of Marriage: Facing the Complexities of Commitment with the Wisdom of God* (New York: Penguin, 2011), 95.

3. Child Welfare Information Gateway, *Understanding the Effects of Maltreatment on Brain Development* (Washington, DC: US Department of Health and Human Services, Children's Bureau, 2015), https://www .childwelfare.gov/pubPDFs/brain_development.pdf.

4. The speaker-listener technique was developed by Howard J. Markman, Scott M. Stanley, and Susan L. Blumberg. See "Talking Safely Without Fighting: The Speaker Listener Technique," in *Fighting for Your Marriage: A Deluxe Revised Edition of the Classic Best Seller for Enhancing Marriage and Preventing Divorce*, 3rd ed. (San Francisco: Jossey-Bass, 2010), 106–33.

5. Keller, *The Meaning of Marriage*, 44.

Chapter Ten: Fight Fair and Forgive Often

1. Ellie Lisitsa, "The Four Horsemen: Criticism, Contempt, Defensiveness, and Stonewalling," *The Gottman Relationship Blog* (blog), The Gottman Institute, April 23, 2013, https://www.gottman.com/blog/the-four -horsemen-recognizing-criticism-contempt-defensiveness-and-stone walling/.

2. John M. Gottman and Nan Silver, *The Seven Principles for Making Marriage Work* (New York: Three Rivers, 1999), 31.

3. Gottman and Silver, *Seven Principles*, 31.

4. Aaron Karmin, "How Long Does the Fight or Flight Reaction Last?," *Anger Management* (blog), Psych Central, accessed January 7, 2019, https://blogs.psychcentral.com/anger/2016/06/how-long-does-the-fight -or-flight-reaction-last/.

5. Gottman and Silver, *Seven Principles*, 100.

6. Gottman and Silver, *Seven Principles*, 100.

7. Ted L. Huston, "What's Love Got to Do with It? Why Some Marriages Succeed and Others Fail," *Personal Relationships* 16, no. 3 (2009): 301–27.

8. Linda J. Waite et al., *Does Divorce Make People Happy? Findings from a Study of Unhappy Marriages* (New York: Institute for American Values, 2002), http://americanvalues.org/catalog/pdfs/does_divorce_make_peo ple_happy.pdf.

9. Timothy Keller, *The Meaning of Marriage: Facing the Complexities of Commitment with the Wisdom of God* (New York: Penguin, 2011), 44–45.

10. C. S. Lewis, *The Four Loves* (New York: Harcourt, 1971), 121.

11. Henri Nouwen, *With Open Hands*, 2nd rev. ed. (Notre Dame, IN: Ave Maria, 2006), 92–93.

12. Loren Toussaint, Everett Worthington, and David R. Williams, eds., *Forgiveness and Health: Scientific Evidence and Theories Relating Forgiveness to Better Health* (New York: Springer, 2015), 11, 20.

13. Ashley Heintzelman et al., "Recovery from Infidelity: Differentiation of Self, Trauma, Forgiveness, and Posttraumatic Growth Among Couples in Continuing Relationships," *Couple and Family Psychology: Research and Practice* 3, no. 1 (2014): 13–29.

14. Lewis B. Smedes, *Forgive and Forget: Healing the Hurts We Don't Deserve* (San Francisco: HarperOne, 1996), 133.

Chapter Eleven: Play Together

1. Paul R. Amato et al., *Alone Together: How Marriage in America Is Changing* (Cambridge: Harvard University Press, 2007), 4.

2. Juliet Schor, *The Overworked American: The Unexpected Decline of Leisure* (New York: Basic, 1993), 4.

3. Stuart Brown, *Play: How It Shapes the Brain, Opens the Imagination, and Invigorates the Soul* (New York: Avery, 2010), 5.

4. Brown, *Play*, 17.

5. Arthur Aron et al., "Couples' Shared Participation in Novel and Arousing Activities and Experienced Relationship Quality," *Journal of Personality and Social Psychology* 78, no. 2 (2000): 273–84.

6. Sharon Jayson and *USA Today*, "Married Couples Who Play Together Stay Together," ABC News, July 16, 2008, http://abcnews.go.com /Health/Family/story?id=5387217&page=1.

7. Staci Albrechtsen, "Couples That Play Together Stay Together," Brigham Young University, accessed January 7, 2019, https://foreverfamilies.byu .edu/Pages/couples-that-play-stay.

8. Lawrence Robinson et al., "The Benefit of Play for Adults: How Play Benefits Your Relationships, Job, Bonding, and Mood," HelpGuide.org,

March 2018, https://www.helpguide.org/articles/mental-health/benefits -of-play-for-adults.htm.

9. "The Power of a Smile," Social Psych Online, May 2, 2017, http://social psychonline.com/2017/05/smile-psychology-science/.

10. Viktor Frankl, *Man's Search for Meaning* (Boston: Beacon, 2006), 43.

Chapter Twelve: Maintain Curiosity

1. Ted L. Huston, "What's Love Got to Do with It? Why Some Marriages Succeed and Others Fail," *Personal Relationships* 16, no. 3 (2009): 301–27.

2. *English Oxford Living Dictionaries*, s.v. "curiosity," accessed January 7, 2019, https://en.oxforddictionaries.com/definition/curiosity.

3. Todd B. Kashdan and John E. Roberts, "Trait and State Curiosity in the Genesis of Intimacy: Differentiation from Related Constructs," *Journal of Social and Clinical Psychology* 23, no. 6 (2004): 792–816.

4. Emily Campbell, "Six Surprising Benefits of Curiosity," *Mind and Body* (blog), *Greater Good Magazine*, September 24, 2015, https://greatergood .berkeley.edu/article/item/six_surprising_benefits_of_curiosity.

5. James W. Carson et al., "Mindfulness-Based Relationship Enhancement," *Behavior Therapy* 35, no. 3 (2004): 471–94.

6. Zach Brittle, "Build Love Maps," *The Gottman Relationship Blog* (blog), The Gottman Institute, March 11, 2015, https://www.gottman.com/blog /build-love-maps/.

7. Rich Nicastro, "Healthy Marriage: The Role of Mutual Curiosity," Strengthen Your Relationship, August 22, 2011, http://www.strengthen yourrelationship.com/healthy-marriage-the-role-of-mutual-curiosity/.

Andrea Gurney, PhD, is a licensed psychologist in private practice and a professor at Westmont College. She was born and raised in New York and completed her BA in psychology at Wheaton College, her MSEd in psychological services at the University of Pennsylvania, and her PhD in psychology at Northeastern University. She completed three years of pre- and postdoctoral training at Harvard Medical School. Dr. Gurney's psychotherapy practice over the last fifteen years has included children, adolescents, adults, couples, and families. An East Coast girl at heart, she enjoys living in Santa Barbara with her husband, two daughters, and playful goldendoodle.